Christianity Rediscovered

VINCENT J. DONOVAN

Holy Ghost Father

"But I am still running, trying to capture that
by which I have been captured."
Philippians 3:12

ORBIS BOOKS
Maryknoll, New York 10545

Fourth Printing, December 1985

I want to thank the editors of the *National Catholic Reporter* for permitting me to use ideas that I first wrote of in their pages years ago. No article of that time is reproduced in the same form in this book, but it was in those articles that I first dared to speak of what is developed here.

I am also grateful to Bill Donovan, Peggy Baumgardner, Matt and Peggy Donovan, Annamae Rietski, Kay Donovan, and Nora Koren for their help in preparing the manuscript of this book.

The Catholic Foreign Mission Society of America (Maryknoll) recruits and trains people for overseas missionary service. Through Orbis Books Maryknoll aims to foster the international dialogue that is essential to mission. The books published, however, reflect the opinions of their authors and are not meant to represent the official position of the society.

Library of Congress Cataloging in Publication Data

Donovan, Vincent J., 1926-
  Christianity rediscovered.

  Originally published: Notre Dame, Ind. : Fides/
Claretian, c1978
  1. Christianity—Essence, genius, nature.
2. Missions. 3. Missions to Masai. I. Title.
BT60.D63 1981   230   81-18992
ISBN 0-88344-096-2 (pbk.)   AACR2

For my family,
from whom I first learned the meaning of love
and sacrifice and loyalty of a community

Contents

Preface to the Second Edition   v

Introduction   1

1. One Hundred Years in East Africa   3

2. The Masai   14

3. A Time to Be Silent and a Time to Think   28

4. A Time to Speak and a Time to Act   41

5. What Do You Think of the Christ?   65

6. The Response   81

7. A Time for Laughter and a Time for Tears   99

8. Churches: The New, the Young, and the Particular   129

9. Signs of the Times   164

10. The Winds of Change   175

An African Creed   200

Preface to the Second Edition

In developing a line of thought in a book, one's hope is that readers will easily discern the main purpose of the book and will react to that basic thought, correcting it, developing it, applying it in ways not foreseen even by the author. A parish priest in the United States remarked that even though *Christianity Rediscovered* was written in an African context, out of African experience, it was clear to him the book was really written about the church in Europe and America. I was gratified it was that clear. I had hoped readers would realize it. But more than that, I had hoped they would be able to take that basic thought and apply it to the church in America and elsewhere in a way that I could never do; that somehow the same principles must apply to the church anywhere. It has been a long time since I began to understand that mission is not a one-way street moving away from the home church to the foreign mission field. The new, the young, and the particular churches of the Third World, spoken of by Vatican II, have something to say, in turn, to the church at large.

A very interesting response to the book has been the observation that there is in it traces of a movement away from the theology of salvation to a new theological stance, a movement not so much articulated in the book as acted out—something like the melody of a new unwritten song that haunts you, with the notes and the words not yet in place. It is there just out of your reach and the melody haunts you because it is not yet complete, but you will recognize the song when it is complete: a new song that many are trying to sing today in place of the ancient hymn of salvation.

The theology of salvation was the theory on which all mission activity was based, out of which that activity flowed. The mission compound with its many necessary buildings was the symbol of that theory and theology. The compound stood for the church, the ark and haven of salvation, the repository of grace, and, indeed, of God. Outside that compound lay the vast area of tribal life and pagan culture empty of all worth and goodness and holiness and salvation. The missionary process was a movement away from tribal and human life and culture to the church where salvation resided. It was a process of salvation from this world and from human life. The sacramental system flowed out of that process, with Baptism serving the urgent function of saving people from that life; Confession, of retrieving them when they had fallen back into it; Communion, of protecting them, especially their bodies, against that life; Holy Orders, of lifting them above that life completely, and Extreme Unction, of bidding farewell finally and with some relief to that life.

And whether in the mission field or on the home front one cannot rest one's missionary eyes. Missionaries looking at the church in America would be worried by what they see. Because what they see is a bad missionary situation. Not just the sharp decline in active participation in church community and the draining away of the young, but a church life that is not much more relevant to the human life lived in the neighborhoods surrounding it than the mission compound was to the tribal life of the Africans. The parish church could very well be the mission compound of the American scene, a beleaguered, outpost colony in an alien world.

Baptism, Eucharist, Matrimony, and the Anointing of the Sick in America have become more attractive liturgical ceremonies, but their meaning for human life in this time and place seems to elude us. Defined by Augustine, put into doctrinal form by Aquinas, counted by the Council of Trent, the sacraments seem to have come to the end of the process of exploration and discovery. Despite the flurry of books since Vatican II, there has been no systematic treatment or study of the sacraments, as desperately as it is needed. They become more and more unreal. Confirmation is in a limbo of uncertainty. People, voting with their feet, have all but eliminated Confession, and with it, penance and the forgiveness that haunts the pages of the New Testament. The ministry of the church is still being based on the very doubtful future of the dwindling vocations of the seminaries. Christian communities are being closed down. Pastoral positions are being filled with a flow of priests from outside the country. Almost any solution is being considered except the one that would make us face, as honestly as possible, the authentic meaning and implications of New Testament ministry.

Evangelization is a process of bringing the gospel to people where they are, not where you would like them to be. And where they are in America is at a stage somewhere between a faith and a religion. You have to respect that stage of belief as much as you would respect the stage of belief of a pagan tribe, without necessarily admitting that either one is Christianity, or the church as it should be.

Evangelization in America presents many different and interesting challenges. In this book I describe work among a famous African tribe. I realized, when I came back to America, that here on the home front I had left behind me one of the most exotic tribes of all—the young people of America. They have their own form of dress symbolized by the omnipresent blue jeans; their own food, not always the most nutritious; their own music, which, I confess, I do not understand; their own rituals enacted as they listen to their music in concert; their own language, their own values remarkably similar from New York to California. Dress, food, music, ritual, language, values—these are the things that make up a tribe, or a sub-culture as they have been called. It is to that tribe, as they are, that the gospel must be brought.

A young person in an American university, reflecting on the line of thought presented in this book, offered some advice: "In working with young people in America, do not try to call them back to where they were, and do not try to call them to where you are, as beautiful as that place might seem to you. You must have the courage to go with them to a place that neither you nor they have ever been before." Good missionary advice, and a beautiful description of the unpredictable process of evangelization, a process leading to that new place where none of us has ever been before.

When the gospel reaches a people where they are, their response to that gospel is the church in a new place, and the song they will sing is that new, unsung song, that unwritten melody that haunts all of us. What we have to be involved in is not the revival of the church or the reform of the church. It has to be nothing less than what Paul and the Fathers of the Council of Jerusalem were involved in for their time—the refounding of the Catholic church for our age.

Two things must come together to lead us to that new place—the gospel and the sacred arena of people's lives. What we referred to tentatively in Africa as the naked gospel, what Karl Rahner describes theologically as the "final and fundamental substance of the Christian message," must be brought to bear on the real flesh and blood world in which we live. The result, I think, could be a new church in a new place, a new ministry of the priesthood of all believers, away from the temple, far from the altar and sanctuary, out in the midst of human life as it is lived in the neighborhoods, in the teeming, forlorn city; a ministry of politics and law, a ministry of commerce, a ministry of sports and entertainment and music, a ministry of human life and love; a ministry in which all of life and all of the world would be offered up with the bread and wine. All this is my body.

The premise of this book is that every theology or theory must be based on previous missionary experience, and that any theory or theology which is not based on previous experience is empty words, of use to no one. The conviction of the book is the belief that the gospel itself, untied to any social service or other inducement, is a message filled with power and fertility and creativity and freedom. The main thrust of the book describes an attempt to empower a particular people with the freedom and total responsibility of that gospel. This experience, lived out in the lonely pastoral setting of the Masai steppes of East Africa, is far removed from the spreading urban-technological society in which we live. Can the experience of the one world be of any value to the other? I do not know. I can only say the cry of hopelessness I heard then in that desert setting is not much different from the cry I hear today in the wasteland of our cities.

The prophet Micah heard the city of Jerusalem, the gathering place for all the tribes and nations, crying aloud. He urged it to continue crying so that someone might respond to that cry. "Cry out, daughter of Zion," he said, "the Lord himself will hear you." The cry of Jerusalem is the cry of the city today. It is the cry of the church, the new Jerusalem. It is the cry of all the tribes and nations of the earth yearning to be filled at the messianic banquet table. The cry of Jerusalem is the cry of creation groaning and travailing even until now, waiting for the revelation of the sons and daughters of God. "Preach the gospel to all creation," Christ said. Are we only now beginning to understand what he meant? I believe the unwritten melody that haunts this book ever so faintly, the new song waiting to be sung in place of the hymn of salvation, is simply the song of creation. To move away from the theology of salvation to the theology of creation may be the task of our time.

—*Vincent J. Donovan*

Introduction

Evangelism is not the most popular subject in the church today, the church of the post-Vatican II era. Conversion, to most people, no longer means "metanoia." It means rather proselytism and is a pejorative word. Missionary work, which involves taking the message of Christ to people who do not believe in him, who indeed have never heard of him, thus becomes a distasteful task. Many misgivings, fears, and suspicions revolve around the whole missionary movement and missionary history—the violence done to the cultures, customs, and consciousness of peoples, the callousness and narrow-mindedness found in that history. The author of this book was involved in all of that.

I wonder if it would remove some of the misgivings if the reader would understand that that is precisely what this book is all about. Suppose *you* were a missionary and you realized how questionable the whole system was. And yet suppose you believed in Christianity, believed that Christianity had something to say to the world that is pagan—for that is what it is, more than three-quarters pagan. What then? What would you do?

Maybe you would do as we did, begin all over again from the beginning. That means precisely what it says, starting from the beginning, with, perhaps, only one conviction to guide you, a belief that Christianity is of value to the world around it. That is presumption enough. Beyond that, no preconceived ideas either as to what Christianity is or what paganism is. What it means is a willingness to search honestly for that Christianity and to be open to those pagan cultures; to bring Christianity and paganism together and see what happens, if anything happens;

1

to see what emerges if anything can emerge, without knowing what the end result will be.

The actual carrying out of such a quest has been an adventure, a journey of the mind and of the soul, a disconcerting, disturbing, shattering, humbling journey. I would like to invite the reader to go on that journey with me. But before commencing it, one would want to have the same open-mindedness toward it, with no convictions beyond the one that Christianity is something of value; no preconceived notions about God, salvation, Christ, the meaning of being a Christian, the church, the sacraments, the liturgy, the priesthood, or anything else traditionally associated with Christianity. Without such an openness of mind on the part of the reader, this book would make no sense.

I believe that this particular journey is a voyage of discovery. But how to communicate that discovery, how to share it with others? A participant in a discovery such as this will feel none of the elation and contentment found by a mathematician whose discovery can be satisfactorily demonstrated to his colleagues, nor any of that found in a doctor or a scientist whose breakthrough will soon make itself felt in the world. The experience of discovery such as I am describing is rather more like the loneliness of a person who has climbed to a mountain peak and sees spread out around him the most beautiful panoramic vision and vista and finds it completely impossible to describe that vision, or even to discuss it, except with someone who agrees to climb that peak in turn.

1

One Hundred Years in East Africa

Bwaga Moyo

One would think it would be a fairly simple matter to define missionary work, to describe it, to explain its meaning, its purpose, and the methods by which it must be carried out. One would think, also, that a missionary from East Africa, for instance, would find no difficulty in communicating with a colleague working in South America. Both thoughts might be true if missionary work had not been carried out in history. But history has ensured that communication is virtually impossible between the aforementioned missionaries. And history has offered the opportunity to deflect and distort the meaning of missionary work in every age.

History, of course, has also offered us the opportunity to understand better the mission of the church, but for some reason we have rarely availed ourselves of this opportunity. The history of East Africa in modern times, an era that coincides with the time of the missions in that area, is a good example. Right from the beginning of the missions in East Africa there have been factors at work which have deflected missionary work from true center and which leave us today, in any discussion on the matter, floundering on the periphery.

Consider the problem facing the first missionaries who came to East Africa just over a century ago: slavery. It is not easy for us, so far removed in time from that period, to imagine the dimensions of the problem. Before slavery, as a system, came to East Africa, the people had an orderly, fairly stable way of life. But when the Arab slave traders and their European backers arrived on the scene, they brought havoc and confusion and

3

misery unimaginable. There was scarcely a section or a tribe of East Africa that was not affected by it in one way or another. Anarchy took the place of the order that was once the life of the East African tribes. The Arab raiders went far inland to get their slaves and they drove them back to the coast toward Zanzibar. The last stop on the mainland was Bagamoyo.[1]

It is said that Bagamoyo takes its name from the two Swahili words, *bwaga* and *moyo*. *Bwaga* means to *throw down*, or *put down*, or *let down*. In a long safari, the one leading the safari, at different points, would yell to the porters, *"Bwaga mizigo,"* "put down your loads." *Moyo* means heart. *Bwaga moyo* would thus mean, "Put down your heart." Bagamoyo was the place where the captured slave, after his long trip from the interior, would put down his heart, lay down the burden of his heart, give up hope—because it was his last contact with his own country before the trip to Zanzibar and a life of misery.

It is easy to understand the feeling of the missionaries who arrived on the scene in the last century, their concern with doing something about the system of slavery which was the cause of all these horrors. They did the only thing they could in the circumstances. They bought the slaves. They bought them left and right, with all the money they could get their hands on. They bought them by the hundreds and by the thousands—and they christianized all they bought. Buying slaves and christianizing them became, in fact, the principal method of the apostolate not only in East Africa, but on the entire continent. There were exceptions to this method, such as the work in Uganda, which was begun some time after that in Zanzibar and Bagamoyo.[2]

Money for this vast enterprise was supplied by Rome, by Protestant missionary societies, and by antislavery societies in Europe and America. The missionaries were, in good conscience, fighting the system of slavery. But in looking back, one wonders if the best way to fight a system was to buy the products of that system.

The missionaries bought those slaves, took care of them and fed them by means of huge farms and plantations, run by the ex-slaves themselves. One would feel reassured if the missionary journals of that time showed evidence that the lot of the ex-slaves was noticeably better than that of their slave counterparts on Zanzibar or elsewhere. Physical cruelty, of course, was never part of the mission compound regime. But the word "free" might not be the most accurate word to describe life on the mission plantations. And even for that freedom, such as it was, there was a price to be paid—acceptance of the Christian religion.

One wonders how many missionaries of the time questioned the wisdom of what they were doing. Because what they were doing was sheer folly. They were trying to build the church in the most artificial way imaginable. Following baptism of these ex-slaves, and the training of many of them in the work-shop schools, the mission arranged marriages among them, hoping to settle them as Christian families and villages on some part of the vast "mission compound." According to the normal rate of progression, by our time a century later, the number of Christians descended from these ex-slaves should have reached gigantic proportions. But just the opposite is true. Their number is negligible in East Africa. The apostolate to the slaves had been a miserable failure.

But perhaps more serious in the long run—this early missionary effort in East Africa has left its subtle mark, the mark of slavery, on all succeeding generations of missionary work. The mission compounds are still in evidence in East Africa. And the questionable motivation for baptism, the subservience and dependence of the christianized peoples, the condescension of the missionaries, are themes that have returned again and again in the intervening hundred years. And the distortion as to the purpose and meaning and methods of missionary work has taken us far from true center.

Bagamoyo stands like a ghost town today, with its huge and empty cathedral, its slave blockhouse, its tall coconut trees with their branches hardly stirring in the stupefying heat, and its melancholy graveyard filled with the remains of so many young missionaries, with the sleep of a century upon them.

Bwaga moyo indeed—"leave here your heart and hopes," a fitting symbol for the thousands of slaves, the many missionaries, and a half-century of missionary work in Africa.

Up From Slavery

There was one man who was worried about the apostolate to the slaves—as far as missionary work was concerned—and did something about it. Just after the turn of the century, about the year 1906, Joseph Shanahan, bishop of Southern Nigeria, took money which was coming from Propaganda in Rome, money sent specifically to ransom slaves, and used it to begin the building of the extensive school system of Southern Nigeria. He not only affected the destiny of a tribe, the Ibos; he helped to change the missionary history of all of Africa. A new era began in the African missions with Bishop Shanahan.[3]

Not long after Bishop Shanahan, both East and West Africa took up the school system as a new apostolic method. The schools were not much to begin with, mostly catechetical or bush schools, where reading, writing, and religion were taught. Religion was the main subject. And the main character on the scene was the catechist. He became the mainstay of every mission compound. He was usually a dedicated and good-living man, not young, and not trained. One aspect of the apostolate to the slaves carried over into the catechetical period—an emphasis on children, the parents of tomorrow. The catechist has persisted on the East African mission scene even until the present time— but with nothing of his former importance. An alarming fact was noted in a survey which was made in the early sixties, a survey which covered all of East Africa. It was the fact that ninety percent of all religious instruction was being given, not by the missionary or the priest, but by the catechist. Even in this directly religious task, preaching the gospel such as it was, the missionary was not immediately involved, was not at the center, but was off somewhere in the periphery. But worse than that, these untrained catechists were ignorant of the true Christian message, and they passed on their ignorance to others. It was not a comforting thought in the early sixties to realize that a major portion of the edifice of the church and of Christianity in East Africa rested on that shaky foundation.[4]

The catechetical schools gradually developed into schools of secular learning; into primary schools, middle schools, secondary schools, teachers' training colleges. The battle of the schools was on. Catholics and Protestants joined earnestly in the battle. It is hard for someone who was not there during that time to understand the intensity and bitterness of the struggle. Whoever got the schools in a certain area was sure to get the Christians who came out of those schools. The basic premise underlying all of this was that if children entered a mission school, they would not emerge from that school without being Christians. And the premise was essentially correct.

Now, in the place of the catechist, the teacher of secular subjects became the main figure on mission compounds and in mission out-stations. He became the right hand of the missionary and the instrument of missionary policy. It is no exaggeration to say that the school became *the* missionary method of East Africa. This was a policy eagerly backed by Rome. In 1928, Monsignor Hinsley, Apostolic Visitor to East Africa, told a gathering of bishops in Dar es Salaam: "Where it is impossible for you to carry on both the immediate task of evangelization and your educational work, neglect your churches in order to perfect your schools."[5]

Young missionaries followed that advice and spent their lives acquiring, building up, supplying, and teaching in schools of every description. This activity continued down into the sixties. There is no doubt about it, it was a heady experience being in the forefront of an adventure that was bringing education on an enormous scale, to what was then called an underdeveloped country.

But to return to the original question of this book: what is the purpose and meaning of missionary work? Once again, historical factors had intervened and thrown out of focus the essential notions of this important issue. I think few missionaries of the time of the educational apostolate could have given a straightforward answer to the question.

The colonial governments were slow to recognize the value of the school system, or perhaps were afraid of its implications. At any rate, it can be truly said that the school system of East Africa was the creation, by and large, of the mission. Eventually the governments did move in on the educational field, and with increasingly feverish activity as independence neared, tried to take over more and more of the program. But they had a late start. At the time of independence in Tanganyika, for instance, in the year 1961, seventy percent of all the schools in the country were still being run by the missions.

By the time independence came to the three East African countries, the missions had come to maturity. All three leaders of these countries had been educated in mission schools, and two of them continued to be professing Christians. The parliaments of all three countries were filled with Christian legislators. The number of Christians had grown to sizeable and representative proportions of the countries involved. Education was not the only benefit Christianity had brought to Africa. Western medicine and other elements of civilization had penetrated the most remote areas. There was reason for immense satisfaction in looking at the credit side of the missionary ledger.

But let us look at the debit side:

1) Missionary and church work had become even more child-oriented than ever it was in the slavery and catechetical days. 2) Religion had become a subject taught in the school, similar to mathematics or Swahili. 3) Liturgy had been entirely neglected.

4) After close to a hundred years of the church's presence in the country, the first African bishop was set up as an Ordinary in a diocese of Tanganyika, in the very year of independence. There was none in Kenya. 5) African clergy, numerous among certain tribes, were few in proportion to the overall number of Christians. In the important and large diocese of Nairobi, there was only one African priest. Such African priests as there were had become, through their training, almost completely un-African, and extremely conservative and suspicious of any change. 6) In this educational period, an old familiar price had come to be exacted from those who sought a new freedom, freedom from ignorance—and that price was the acceptance of Christianity. 7) As far as the Christianity itself was concerned, an inward-turned, individual-salvation-oriented, unadapted Christianity had been planted in Africa. 8) The Christian churches were made up of subservient, dependent people. As far as finances went, there was scarcely a diocese or a parish that could have stood on its own, without continued outside support. 9) The Holy Ghost Fathers, the White Fathers, the Maryknoll Fathers, the Capuchins, and the Benedictines were firmly established in East Africa, but it is doubtful if the church was. Mission compounds resembled nothing so much as foreign outposts. 10) Missionaries, who should have had pride and contentment in their accomplishments, were in the greatest quandary of all. Few of them had really wanted independence to come, and when it had, many of them had lost their nerve, their sense of direction and purpose. 11) The newly independent governments were to become increasingly jealous of the schools as their prerogative, and by 1970 all mission schools in the new Tanzania,[6] for instance, were taken over completely by the government. By this one swift move the government was to rob the missionaries of their main apostolic method, and to render the advice of that Apostolic Visitor of 1928 hollow indeed. 12) Finally, the meaning and purpose of missionary work had been so thoroughly distorted

that it was scarcely recognizable. Missionaries were at a loss to describe meaningful missionary methods in the existing situation.

A badly deteriorating situation almost received its "coup de grace" from the turbulent events of the sixties.

Whither Mission?

Among the first ones to jump into the void of missionary thinking were the African leaders of newly independent countries. Very capable and thinking men, these leaders addressed themselves time and time again to the missionaries in their countries. They lectured them on the meaning of missionary work. Thanking them for their past contributions, they reminded them that the day of the school apostolate and the medical apostolate were swiftly passing away, and they called on them for a new missionary contribution. They invited them to take part in the battle against ignorance, poverty, and disease. They encouraged them to take an important part in nation building and in aid to developing countries of the third world, as they were now known. They asked them to be servants of these developing countries, to serve under the respective governments of these countries, to help them carry out their policies both internal and sometimes even foreign—as regards Rhodesia, Portugal, and South Africa. They were specifically invited to be "agricultural missionaries" in one country. The president of another East African country was actually asked to address the General Chapter of one missionary congregation, involved in the up-dating of its missionary aims and purpose. There is no doubt that he influenced that congregation tremendously. The similarity, even to wording, between his speech and their new guidelines is remarkable.[7]

One cannot doubt the intelligence nor the sincerity of these African leaders. They are extraordinary men, and any mission-

ary who has even had contact with them, cannot but feel a deep
admiration for them. And they can give us a deep insight into
the aspirations and needs of the African people. They can even
serve as signs of the times for us. But the question still must be
asked: When we are searching for the deepest biblical and
theological meaning of missionary work, is it to statesmen and
politicians that we should turn for the answer?

The decade of the sixties was also the time of the Second
Vatican Council and its aftermath. One of the most important
discussions of that assembly was the debate on the mission of the
church. It was a very intense debate, which tension does not fully
appear in the finished documents of the Council.[8] It was a debate over whether the deepest meaning of the mission of the
church concerned itself with the evangelization of pagan
peoples, or with the reevangelization of Christian peoples.
There were some firm principles enunciated with regard to the
primacy of first evangelization, as it was called, but there was also
compromise allowed when it came down to spelling out the all-
important distinction between missionary and pastoral work. In
another important section of the Council proceedings, the
Catholic church went on record for the first time in its history in
support of true freedom of conscience and tolerance for other
religions. Every missionary was grateful for the immense
amount of light thrown on the missionary situation by the Second Vatican Council.

But shortly after the Council, one began to hear such state-
ments as, "France is the mission. Holland is the mission," or,
"Chicago is as much mission as Nairobi." Young Dutch members
of missionary congregations began to desire to be missionaries to
the Dutch, to the people of their own country, especially the
young, who needed them as much as any people in foreign
mission stations ever would.

Then the voice of tolerance began to be heard questioning
missionary work among peoples of non-Christian religions. This
voice insisted that it was a violation of conscience to convert any

people from their own beliefs to beliefs of your choosing. Finally from all of this there emerged the new definition of missionary work: aid to developing countries, material help to these countries without any strings attached. Conversion was out of the question. A new breed of missionaries appeared—behind the plow, laying pipes, digging wells, introducing miracle grains, bringing progress and development to the peoples of the third world—a kind of ecclesiastical peace corps. This is the new and exciting meaning of missionary work and of missionaries—a discovery of our time.[9]

I wonder if one would be allowed to ask what is new about it. Material development? Isn't that what was involved from the beginning in the work in East Africa, with the freed slaves, the workshops, the plantations, and in the building and running of schools? Perhaps the only thing new about it is the machinery available today, and the motivation of the missionaries.

By the very nature of the case, this new breed of missionaries must condemn the previous system of missionary work—and one would have to agree with them in their condemnation. To bring freedom or knowledge or health or prosperity to a people *in order that* they become Christians is a perversion of missionary work. But what of a system that would bring them progress and development for its own sake? Is that not just as bad? Nazism will stand forever as the ultimate indictment of progress for its own sake. How would a Christian missionary involved in such work be differentiated from agents of socio-economic systems such as communism or socialism, or even from workers for the United Nations? Or should no such differentiation be made, as some insist? Have we come to the end of the era of the mission? Are they no more relevant than the British Foreign Office for colonial administration?

Or is it possible that *none* of the systems already described throw essential light on the true meaning of missionary work?

There is no mistaking the fact that missionary work is in a shambles. Born in slavery, disoriented by the school system, startled by independence, and smothered in nation building—mission in East Africa has never had the chance to be true to itself.

To make any sense out of mission, out of the meaning and purpose of missionary work, one has to start all over again—at the beginning.

NOTES TO CHAPTER 1

1. Bagamoyo mission, together with the mission on Zanzibar, represent the first missionary steps into East and Central Africa in modern times. Bagamoyo was a famous mission, known to all the explorers of the time, and was the starting point for such men as Livingstone and Stanley.

2. In 1878, eighteen years after the Holy Ghost Fathers had begun working in Zanzibar and Bagamoyo, the White Fathers, organized and supplied at the mission of Bagamoyo, set out for Nyassa and Uganda. Cf. Henry J. Koren, C.S. Sp., *The Spiritans: A History of the Congregation of the Holy Ghost* (Duquesne University Press, 1958), p. 197.

3. Koren, *The Spiritans,* p. 466, pp. 531 ff.

4. A private survey on the state of religious education in East Africa drawn up by Rev. Adrian Hastings in 1960.

5. Judith Listowel, *The Making of Tanganyika* (London: Chatto and Windus, 1965), p. 102.

6. Tanganyika and the Island of Zanzibar joined in the United Republic of Tanzania in April of 1964, the name Tanzania being formed from the original titles of the two previously independent countries.

7. Julius K. Nyerere, "Speech to the Maryknoll Congress in New York" (Dar es Salaam: Government Printer, 1970).

8. Walter M. Abbot, S.J., *The Documents of Vatican Two* (America Press, 1966), pp. 580–582, 592.

9. A whole new dimension was added to the modern definition of missionary at a later time, when the theologians of liberation appeared on the scene.

2

The Masai

Letter to a Bishop

Loliondo Mission
May 1966

Dear Bishop,

As you know, I have been in this mission of Loliondo scarcely a year. It certainly is the most interesting and exotic mission in the diocese, located, as it is, deep in the heart of Masailand, bordering the Serengeti plains, the big game paradise of Tanzania, and of East Africa.

I wonder if I could make some comments on the mission. There are four well-run, well-looked-after, expensive, nonaided schools attached to the mission. There is a small chapel. There is a hospital, extremely well built, fairly well attended, bringing in some mission revenue. The hospital and school take up an enormous amount of time, especially the hospital. It is common practice for the mission car, when it is called for, to pick up sick people at a distance and to bring them to the hospital, expenses being paid by the sick. This is happening on the average of once a week, with one of the priests in the mission doing the driving. In our four schools, religious instruction is for all students in the school. There is also religious instruction for many students in the government school, in the village of Loliondo. The influence of the Catholic Mission is very strong in the whole Loliondo area, certainly much stronger than that of any other agency, government or otherwise. But the relationships with the Masai people have to do with schools, hospitals, or cattle. Many of the Masai have been helped materially by the mission. There are many instances of strong friendship-relationship between the Masai and the priests in the mission.

Masai kraals are visited very often. All important events in Masai life,

14

such as circumcision, are attended by the priests. Milk and honey beer are drunk. The priests even sleep in Masai kraals.

But never, or almost never, is religion mentioned on any of these visits. The best way to describe realistically the state of this Christian mission is the number zero. As of this month, in the seventh year of this mission's existence, there are no adult Masai practicing Christians from Loliondo mission. The only practicing Christians are the catechist and the hospital medical dresser, who have come here from other sections of Masailand.

That zero is a real number, because up until this date no Catholic child, on leaving school, has continued to practice his religion, and there is no indication that any of the present students will do so.

The relationship with the Masai, in my opinion, is dismal, time consuming, wearying, expensive, and materialistic. There is no probability that one can speak with the Masai, even with those who are our friends, about God. And there is no likelihood that one could actually interest them to the point of their wanting to discuss or accept Christianity.

In other words, the relationship with the Masai, except the school children, goes into every area except that very one area which is most dear to the heart of the missionary. On this one important point, there is no common ground with the Masai. It looks as if such a situation will go on forever. Indeed I have heard one missionary say that it may take one hundred years before the Masai are willing and ready to talk with us about God, but we must stay here so that we will be present when that day comes.

Looking at these people around me, at these true pagans, I am suddenly weary of the discussions that have been going on for years in the mission circles of Europe and America, as to the meaning of missionary work, weary of the meetings and seminars devoted to missionary strategy.

I suddenly feel the urgent need to cast aside all theories and discussions, all efforts at strategy—and simply go to these people and do the work among them for which I came to Africa.

I would propose cutting myself off from the schools and the hospital, as far as these people are concerned—as well as the socializing with them—and just go and talk to them about God and the Christian message.

I know this is a radical departure from traditional procedure, but the very fact that it be considered so shows the state we are in.

The expense for running this mission last year came close to a quarter of a million shillings. Just the maintenance of the cars driving over these unbelievable roads is staggering, but it is still considered justified because of the school supplies that are carried, and the sick who are brought to the hospital. Would everyone in the diocese consider the same travel expenses justified if the safaris in the car were made to carry nothing—except the missionary—to go to people to do nothing but to talk to them about Christ? I'm not so sure that everyone would consider such expenses justified. Which once again shows you what state we are in.

But that is precisely what I would propose to do. I know what most people say. It is impossible to preach the gospel directly to the Masai. They are the hardest of all the pagans, the toughest of the tough. In all their hundreds of years of existence, they have never accepted anything from the outside. You cannot bring them the gospel without going through several preparatory, preliminary stages.

But I would like to try. I want to go to the Masai on daily safaris— unencumbered with the burden of selling them our school system, or begging for their children for our schools, or carrying their sick, or giving them medicine.

Outside of this, I have no theory, no plan, no strategy, no gimmicks— no idea of what will come. I feel rather naked. I will begin as soon as possible.

> *Sincerely,*
> *Vince Donovan*

The People

How does one go about describing the Masai[1]—the most glamorous and written-about people in East Africa? I have seen few Europeans who have come across the Masai who have not gone away with a deep feeling of admiration and affection for them. It is hard to explain their attraction. Their history is not

known like that of the Zulus of South Africa—with even the
times and places of their battles recorded for history. Masai history, as much as it can be reconstructed, is pieced together from
the horror stories of the surrounding Bantu tribes. But unlike
the Zulus, the Masai are still there in all their glory, living basically the same life they were leading before the Europeans
landed on the coast. Unlike the Zulus they have never been
conquered. They have been repulsed from time to time by
people like the fierce Wahehe, but never conquered. So they
have that unmistakable, exasperating air of invincibility, of a
superiority complex, about them. One has to see them suddenly
silhouetted against the horizon, tall, spare, proud, leaning on
their shields and spears and staring silently across the plains, to
catch a glimpse of that wisp of history still being lived.

They are spread over thirty thousand square miles of Tanzania, some sixty or seventy thousand strong.[2] An accurate cen-
sus is not easy to come by. Besides the fact that they are
seminomadic, often on the move, it would need a stout-hearted
census-taker to reach all their isolated and far-flung cattle
kraals, right through the heart of lion and warrior infested
country.

The heart of the Masai culture is the warrior class (*il murran*),
guardians of the flocks and of the tribe itself. Insolent, vain, and
incredibly courageous, these young men enter their majority on
the day they are circumcised. All those circumcised within a
certain time span belong to the same age group (*orporor*), the
most outstanding class distinction and most important cultural
value in the tribe. The circumcision itself is their first test, and it
is a real one. The slightest flinching of eyes or face or twitching
of muscles or arm or leg during the circumcision ceremony
would entail a lifelong social ostracism. For close on fifteen years
after their circumcision these *murran* have no responsibility except defense of the tribal herds and enlarging of the herds
through cattle theft. It is not really thieving. All cattle in the
world belong to the Masai by divine right. So it is just a question

of returning the cattle to their proper owners. The warriors are not allowed to get married, nor are they encouraged to take part in the councils of the tribes. There is, therefore, a great deal of sexual freedom allowed between warriors and unmarried girls. The dances of the young people, indeed, of the Masai in general, are very spartan, almost military in style. The grunt of the lion repeated in chorus by the male dancers serves as the rhythm of their singing. The lion is much admired.

Living in the midst of the last great concentration of wild game left in the world, they have worked out a system of peaceful coexistence with the animals. They do not eat wild meat, therefore they do not hunt it. But the lion remains a constant danger and challenge. He is a threat to their herds, and they are willing to take on a lion, in groups or singlehandedly, with the aid of their razor-sharp knives or six foot spears. To kill a lion, for a Masai, as difficult and dangerous as such a test is, is sure proof of adulthood and manhood, and a guarantee that he does not have to spend the rest of his life trying to prove that he has grown up.

At the end of their warriorhood, a whole age group of murran goes through the *eunoto* ceremony—the entrance to elderhood. They cut off their pigtails, the sign of warriorhood, have their last bachelor get-togethers, and build a house called *osinkira*, which symbolically represents their wives. After their last meal together, a specially prepared black bull, they rise up on the horizon and race screaming to the osinkira, which is defended by the elders, reluctant to allow this group into the responsible leadership of the tribe. Running several miles across the plains towards the house, with tears streaming down their faces for the first time in their lives, they are running their youth away. When they reach that house, they will no longer be young. They will be elders, eligible now for ownership of cattle and for marriage.

The leadership of the tribe, conducted by the elders, is democratic in the extreme. There has never been a paramount chief of the calibre of Shaka, king of the Zulus, or the Kabaka of the Baganda. Each section of the Masai has its own leader. He does not reach that position by political maneuvering or personal ambition. He is chosen for his excellence, for the qualities deemed necessary to lead his section and to arbitrate difficulties. It can truly be said he does not even want the job. He is called *legwanan,* and it is his job for life. It is all very symbolic. The legwanan is considered the one who will be first in battle, first to own cattle, first to get married and the first to die—all for the sake of his age group.

The girls are circumcised also, but they belong to the age group of the men they marry. Polygamy is the normal way of life for Masai women. But one must be careful about making hasty judgments concerning the status of women in such a social structure. Masai women are far more independent, financially and otherwise, far more influential in the life of the tribe than many other African women. Attractive, healthy, and extremely intelligent, these Masai women will center their lives around the kraals, which they themselves will build and maintain, homes made of sticks and mud and cow dung. They are in charge of the milking of the cows but take no part in the herding. Regular herding is done by uncircumcised boys. There is not much cooking to be learned, since milk is the staple diet of the Masai, sometimes thickened out with blood from the living cow's neck, and sometimes roasted meat.

If the rhythm is supplied by males, it is the girls and women who supply the melody, and much more, to the Masai singing and dancing. They are the heart of it, and the living treasury of the repertoire of Masai music. Girls prefer to have their heads shaved bald, and covered with an ochre and fat mixture for feast days and dancing. They always wear a circular necklace of beads, the more auspicious the occasion, the greater number of rings of beads. The necklaces are reminiscent, and most probably not accidentally so, of the circular neck rings worn by the nobles and pharaohs of ancient Egypt, even as to color combinations chosen by both peoples. Masai women are skilled in the handicraft of leather and bead work. Their use of color in beadwork is not easily imitated. It is not garish or gaudy, but rather surprisingly subtle and sophisticated. They are practiced in the necessary art of keeping milk containers scoured and antiseptic.[3] A Masai woman is a true "mulier fortis," accustomed to a hard, demanding life, remarkably enduring of physical, bodily pain. As in any pagan society, a Masai girl has no official status in her tribe, but she walks tall and proud, conscious of the true power that is in her.

The cow is not sacred in the Eastern Indian sense, but it is sacred in the daily meaning of life. Everything the Masai has comes from the cow—his home of cow dung, his food—milk and beef, his clothes of cow skin, his medium of exchange and wealth. The life of the Masai is certainly determined by the cow, the places of grass and water, the times to burn down the homestead to move on to other pastures. The very form of a Masai kraal is an enclosure for cattle, with homes on the periphery. Any danger to the cattle is a danger to the Masai, and the attraction of herds of neighboring tribes is irresistible.

The Masai is a true pastoralist. Farming is anathema to him. The Masai word for farmer is *olmeg* and is truly a term of opprobrium. He uses it for everything that is non-Masai. For a Masai, the word *olmeg* means Bantu, European, barbarian.

The Masai are not Bantu like the majority of Africans south of the Sahara. They are classified as Nilo-Hamitics, who have a dim remembrance of their origins along the Nile—the last of the Hamite invasion to reach East and Central Africa.

There is no future tense in the Masai language. Tomorrow will be like today. The Masai are utter conservatives, afraid of change of any kind. They are practically the only tribe in Tanzania that has been exposed to every kind of change, and have successfully resisted it. European clothes, houses, Western education and agriculture have very little value in their eyes.

They have the positive characteristics of pastoralists. They are

hospitable, generous, affectionate, worshipers of children, unbe-
lievably domestic and gentle, and religious. They are firm believers in the one God, *Engai,* but are plagued by a fear of evil
spirits, which fear is exploited by the witch doctor, the laibon.
They have no ancestor worship like most Africans, no belief in
immortality, no burial for the dead. Hyenas fulfill the last
named function.

Bravest of the brave, a warrior tribe living the life they have
led unchanged over these hundreds and hundreds of years.
Neither gatherers of food, nor hunters nor farmers, they are a
sixteenth or seventeenth century people, with tomorrow all
around them, whose today is yesterday.

There is a trace of ancient Egypt in their finely chiseled features, in their slightly slanted eyes, in their reckoning the beginning of any month by the dying of the moon, in their half forgotten customs, and, perhaps, in their blood.

Dressed for all the world like Roman soldiers, red from head
to feet, red tunics, red helmets made of mud, with spear,
shortsword and shield, they stride across the plains and consciousness of Africa, the finest example of what Africa once was.

Ndangoya

Work among the Masai in Tanzania was begun more than
twenty years ago by the Catholic Mission. There are hundreds of
Catholic Masai, but most of them are school boys and all of them
are scattered over thousands and thousands of square miles,
without any vital relationship to each other or to the church of
which they are a part. Many of them, on leaving school after
Standard Four or Standard Seven, return to an environment
that is so foreign to the Christian life, that they are simply swal-
lowed up in paganism, retaining not much more than their
Christian names.

I made my way early one morning with a Masai catechist

named Paul to a carefully selected Masai kraal, the kraal of an influential Masai elder called Ndangoya. I asked Ndangoya if we could speak with him about something very important. He immediately sent for the elders of the three neighboring kraals, and when they arrived, he asked what I wanted to talk about. I said I wanted to talk to them about God, and he answered, "Who can refuse to talk about God?"

I then pointed out that we were well known among the Masai for our work in schools and hospitals, and for our interest in the Masai and their cattle. But now I no longer wanted to talk about schools and hospitals, but about God in the life of the Masai, and about the message of Christianity. Indeed it was for this very work of explaining the message of Christianity to the different peoples of Africa that I came here from far away.

Ndangoya looked at me for a long time, and then said in a puzzled way, "If that is why you came here, why did you wait so long to tell us about this?"

I had no answer for that, but I said I would like, now, at this late date, to explain the Christian message to the Masai people, and I would like to begin here. I wanted the permission of the elders to talk to all the people of the four kraals, who would be interested in listening.

Ndangoya turned to the other elders and talked with them for a few moments. And then he turned to me and said, "Yes, we agree. You may come and talk to all the people. We will let them know, and advise them to come and listen to you, as long as you talk to them here near the kraals, and not far away by your mission house, and as long as you can come here early in the morning at this hour, before we send the cattle out to graze." I agreed to come back the following week and one day every week, and I thanked them for their respectful weighing of my request.

Shortly thereafter, I went to five other sections of Masailand and repeated the process with the elders of those sections. Surprisingly, the question they asked in each section was the same, "Why have you not come to us before?"

Each section agreed to attend the instructions once a week.

Since the only suitable time for instructions was that early morning hour, I could manage only one a day, so most of my working week was filled out. Later on, as I planned to go farther and farther afield across the far-flung parish, where even to reach some of the Masai kraals would require a full day's safari, I began to see the difficulties involved in evangelizing a nomadic people. But as for the present, I could expand no more until I had finished instructions in each of the sections I had begun. And I knew it would take a year to do that. But what if all these distant kraals would accept baptism? What would we do then? How could we possibly take care of them as Christians, and still look to the completion of evangelization in this whole area? Loliondo mission, indeed, the whole notion of mission compound, would be shattered.

I preferred not to look that far into the future. The difficulties of the present were enough, because now that the preliminaries were over, I had to get down to the task of presenting the Masai with the message of Christianity.

Ndangoya was as good as his word. When I returned the following week, he and his colleagues had gathered a very sizeable representation of the four kraals in his neighborhood, to gather to listen to me—both men and women. I certainly did not realize at the time how difficult it was going to be. But as the weeks went by and turned into months, I began to experience the most difficult and tense period of my missionary life.

Here I was, at last, face to face with an adult pagan people, with nothing between me and them but the gospel of Jesus Christ. I knew that beyond this work I was now doing, there were no further moves to make. I was not trying to sell them the school system or Western medicine in order that one day they might accept Christianity. I was trying to convince them directly of the inherent value of Christianity. If I failed here, there would be no going back to some other gimmick to try to draw them once again to receive it. If I failed here, I might as well go home.

I had no way of knowing, no previous experience of myself or of anyone else, how they would react to any point, as step by step I opened and explained the Christian message to these pagans of the pagans.

Each day, in that brisk, early morning hour, still unheated by the equatorial sun, there in the Masai highlands, with the background of the lowing cattle, as I stood waiting for them to gather, I was conscious of the knot in my stomach, wondering if this were the day it would all blow up in my face, with Christianity being utterly rejected by these sons of the plains. Many is the time in that lonely, nomadic setting that I wished I were back in the comfortable company of familiar and acquiescent Christians.

I had to tell them that very first day, when they had all gathered, that I had come to talk about, and deal only with, God. From now on, I would not go in their kraals to sleep, nor would I drink their milk. I would no longer ask for their children for our schools. I wanted no land for mission buildings. I wanted nothing from them. Nor should they expect anything from me. I brought them no gifts, no sweets for the children, no tobacco for the elders, no beads for the women—no medicine for their sick. I had come only to talk about God. They must understand this at the beginning. If they had come for any other motive to listen to me, they must now try to understand.

All of this was rather shocking to them, and unnatural to me. But it was a decision made after much thought. It was not normal, but neither were the previous hundred years of missionary effort normal, and what that effort had led people to believe and expect of missionaries.

Perhaps in all the hundreds and hundreds of years of Masai history, this would be the only opportunity for the Masai to be presented with the bare message of Christianity, untied to any outside influence. I believe that never before in their history had they been presented with such an opportunity—and perhaps never again. For this one, fleeting moment, they should have their chance, and Christianity should have the chance to stand before them in its own unencumbered light.

I told them I believed that they knew about God long before we came, and that they were a devout and very pious people in the face of God. It was not our belief that God loved us Christians more than them, nor that God had abandoned them or forgotten them until we came along. From the beginning it was evident that we were going to have to learn from them as well as teach them.

As I look back on the whole adventure now, I am certain that if I had known the difficulty involved in the process of meeting a pagan people with a Western version of Christianity, I would never have had the courage to begin. Fortunately, my naiveté was boundless. Up until the day of that first instruction I had never spoken to a Masai about God. I had only the most traditional exposition of Christianity to present to them, and not the slightest idea of strategy or missionary principles of first evangelization.

I did not know that there would be whole areas in their life and language that would be blank as far as Christian concepts go—no word in their language for person or creation or grace or freedom or spirit or immortality. There were times in the cold mornings as I faced those nomads when I found myself bitterly resenting the church that had sent me among them, so ill-prepared to deal with them, times when I wondered about the sincerity of that church which styled itself essentially missionary.

Every single thing I prepared to teach them had to be revised or discarded once I had presented it to them. Just what was the essential message of Christianity? What did philosophical reasoning (which we call theology) have to do with it? Had any of those Roman or European theologians, who have given us that theology, ever met a pagan? How much of what we know as morality was involved in the message? What was the church?

As a result of all of this, I know that the original, traditional teaching of Christianity that I presented to them was so revised, adapted, distilled, and filtered in the process that by the end it was hardly recognizable. Now at a point many years later, it is still in the process of revision.

From the moment I decided to take the step into first evangelization, I knew that I would have to begin anew a whole process of study, in any spare time that would be left to me. Scripture, theology, missiology, even anthropology, in any books I could get my hands on, would fill my nights. Safaris would fill my days. Even books on social action would be valuable. One shocking discovery I made was to the effect that there did not seem to exist a single book in the Catholic church on the subject of first evangelization, either as to the methods which might be suited to it, or as to the principles which would govern the work of evangelizing a pagan people.

But perhaps it was just as well there were no books. They would undoubtedly have been like so many of the theology books I had known, treatises woven out of thin air, with little or no relation to life and experience. I was to learn that any theology or theory that makes no reference to previous missionary experience, which does not take that experience into account, is a dead and useless thing. One day the theologians of liberation would say that *praxis* must always be prior to theology. I knew nothing about that at the time. Liberation theology had not yet made its appearance on the ecclesiastical stage. All I knew was that in my work, it would not be a case of going from theory to practice. It would have to be the other way around, a necessity of proceeding from practice to theory. If a theology did emerge from my work, it would have to be a theology growing out of the life and experience of the pagan peoples of the savannahs of East Africa.

I wonder if you ever reach that point in your life or in your work where you are certain you will never have to start all over again.

NOTES TO CHAPTER 2

1. The proper way to refer to the people of this East African tribe, in their own language, is *Il Maásai* with a definite article

and the accent on the first syllable of their name. However, it would be very awkward to do so throughout this book, so I will follow the more common practice of referring to them simply as *the Masai,* as is done in English.

2. Some observers of the scene place their number twice that high. For example, William Redman Duggan and John R. Civille, *Tanzania and Nyerere* (Orbis Books, 1976), p. 11; also, David B. Barrett, *Frontier Situations for Evangelization, 1972: A Survey Report* (Nairobi, Nov. 1973) 36 pp.

3. The normal method of cleansing milk gourds is a vigorous scrubbing with cow urine and red hot charcoal.

3

A Time to Be Silent and a Time to Think

Panta ta Ethne

In America, if I were to walk into a classroom with bad news for one of the students, say a death in his family, he would immediately show shock, then shed tears, and probably run out of the classroom. His culture teaches him to do that.

In the section of Africa where I worked, the results might be just the opposite. A boy being told that his father died, for instance, would show no surprise, no grief, and would continue on with what he was doing, as though nothing had happened. His culture teaches him to do that. It tells him if he really feels sorrow, to grieve in private. It is the same with love. If a young man in Africa really loves a girl, he will speak with other girls in a crowd, flirt with others, even kiss or embrace others. But he will severely ignore in public the girl he loves, if he truly loves her. His culture teaches him to do that.

What about such a basically human thing as the use of words? Surely all human beings would use words in the same way, the way we do. Not so. With us the purpose of words is to take the thought in our minds and put it outside ourselves for everyone to see or hear that thought, a kind of logical use of words.

With these Africans the purpose of words is not to establish logical truth, but to set up social relationships with others. That is quite a difference in the use of words.

As an example, if I were in charge of a boarding school in East Africa and saw a boy break a window in the school, there are two ways I could deal with the situation.

28

I could act out of my own Western culture and call him in and ask, "Johnny, did you break that window?" I want logical truth. He undoubtedly would say, "No," not because he is a liar, but because he is trying, with his words, to repair the social damage I have done with mine.

The second way of dealing with this situation would be to act in consonance with his culture. I could call him in and say,

"Hello, Johnny, how are you?"

"Fine."

"How are you doing in your studies?"

"Better. I'm getting much better marks in math."

"Good, how is your health?"

"Not bad. The food here is good, I'm getting big and strong. I can now kick a football fifty yards. I kicked it through a window."

Culture is all encompassing and all important in the history of salvation. I'm not so certain that is what we were taught before we were sent out here. The church was the receptacle of salvation, and the cultures and nations of the world were the ones to whom salvation was to be doled out by the church.

But you just have to look at the teeming masses of pagans across Africa alone to know there is something wrong with that thought. All these cultures, all these nations outside the pale of salvation, of grace, of holiness, of God's love? Until the church reaches them, if it ever does?

Going back to the New Testament, to that original mandate which sent missionaries all over the world, we find the command of Christ to preach the gospel to all the nations of the world, to disciple, make disciples of, to evangelize all the nations. The words used in the Greek Testament for "all the nations" are *panta ta ethne*. In fact, every time it is mentioned the word "nations" is translated by the Greek word *ethne*. I do not believe that the bible knew of nations in the modern political sense of the word, like the nations of America and Canada and Tanzania.

Ethne would refer more to ethnic, cultural groups, the natural building blocks of the human race. While the political nation of the United States might have very little to do with salvation as such, the Masai culture or a Hindu culture or the cultures that make up America might have very much to do with salvation.

It is surely here in the midst of the cultures of the world, and not in the church, that the ordinary way of salvation must lie, the ordinary means of salvation, the very possibility of salvation for most of the human race. Or else it is a very strange God we have.

The gospel must be brought to the nations in which already resides the possibility of salvation. As I began to ponder the evangelization of the Masai, I had to realize that God enables a people, any people, to reach salvation through their culture and tribal, racial customs and traditions. In this realization would have to rest my whole approach to the evangelization of the Masai.

I had no right to disrupt this body of customs, of traditions. It was the way of salvation for these people, their way to God. It was one of the nations to whom we had to bring the gospel— bring the gospel to it as it was. In those customs lay their possibility of salvation.

Christ himself said, "I did not come to do away with the law (the Jewish culture and religion) but to fulfill it" (Mt 5:17).

Everything concerning a nation (an ethnic cultural group) has to do with salvation. It is the job of the people of that nation, it is their affair to respond to their own call of salvation. It is not the sphere of the evangelist, of the missionary. If we would be consistent, I think we would see that the field of culture is theirs. Ours is the gospel.

An evangelist, a missionary must respect the culture of a people, not destroy it. The incarnation of the gospel, the flesh and blood which must grow on the gospel is up to the people of a culture.

The way people might celebrate the central truths of Christianity; the way they would distribute the goods of the earth and live out their daily lives; their spiritual, ascetical expression of

Christianity if they should accept it; their way of working out the Christian responsibility of the social implications of the gospel—all these things, that is: liturgy, morality, dogmatic theology, spirituality, and social action would be a cultural response to a central, unchanging, supracultural, uninterpreted gospel.

The gospel is, after all, not a philosophy or set of doctrines or laws. That is what a culture is. The gospel is essentially a history, at whose center is the God-man born in Bethlehem, risen near Golgotha.

At that moment facing me was that vast, sprawling, all-pervasive complex of customs and traditions and values and dictates of human behavior which was the Masai culture, a nation in the biblical sense, to whom I had to bring the gospel. At this point I had to make the humiliating admission that I did not know what the gospel was. During those days I spent long hours thinking long, difficult thoughts, and sometimes frightening ones, about the momentous task that faced me—the bringing together of a culture and the gospel.

St. Paul and Mission

To begin thinking about evangelizing the Masai at that time was as difficult as trying to explain it is now. Then and now, the first thing called for is a kind of cleansing of the mind, a beginning with a *tabula rasa* mentality, or something very close to it. This is necessary for a couple of reasons: first, what we will call *first evangelization* is, for all practical purposes, a new field for us. By first evangelization I mean the preaching of the gospel for the first time to any group of people, enabling them to hear for the first time the name of their savior, Jesus. It would encompass the time involved from your very first meeting with any people to talk with them about Christ, up until the time they accept the Christian faith and are baptized, or reject Christ and Christianity. It should be distinguished from the further instruction and guidance needed after baptism for any Christian community until the day when it can stand on its own and you can leave it. The concept of first evangelization lies at the heart of the distinction between missionary and pastoral work. It is directed essentially to people who have never heard of Christ.

The second reason for starting with a clear mind, a mind free of preconceptions, is that there is no other way to deal with a subject that is so strange to us. If we allow our minds and our attitudes to be filled with the convictions and conclusions arising from our pastoral experience, I think we will never arrive at the freedom necessary to make first evangelization possible and understandable.

It was at this point in my searching that I was introduced, by a Lutheran colleague, to the writings of Roland Allen. Roland Allen was an Anglican missionary in China at the beginning of this century. From his experience there, and from his studies, he became convinced that modern missionary methods had strayed far from the missionary methods of the early church, far from the apostolic method. He saw that many of our present day problems in the missions stem from that departure from apostolic method, a departure which led not only to a different way of carrying out mission, but even to a difference in goal, to a difference in the very purpose of mission. He concluded in his classic work, *Missionary Methods: St. Paul's or Ours?* that we today in the missions have something quite different in mind than St. Paul had when he began his famous missionary journeys to carry the gospel into the world outside Jerusalem. His suggestion that we could, with profit, look to the apostolic missionary method as enlightenment and corrective to our own method was like an open door to me. Going through that door was the first step to limitless possibilities. There is probably no point we have reached in our work here, or, in our conclusions, since then, which would agree completely with the thoughts and conclusions of Roland Allen. But I do not think he would have expected us, or wanted us, to come to the identical conclusions on every point that he himself reached over sixty years ago. Our whole world has been transformed, turned upside down, and revolutionized in those sixty years. But the main and general insights and questions of this remarkable man are as valid today as they were when they first stunned and disturbed the church of his day.

Pere Lebbe was a Catholic counterpart to Roland Allen in the Chinese missions, at almost the same time. His thoughts, too, needed years before they gained acceptance in his church. Roland Allen never had the opportunity to carry out and apply his missionary principles in any mission field. If he had the opportunity he undoubtedly would have preferred to apply them among the "highly cultured" peoples of the East, not among the illiterate tribesmen of East Africa. He seemed to display some hesitancy in accepting the validity of these principles as applied to "primitive" peoples. But I am certain that today he would agree to take such a step, taking into consideration the deeper appreciation we have today of the unsuspected richness of the so-called "primitive peoples" of the earth.

Roland Allen's insights and questions challenged most of the missionary theories I had ever heard, and would make it all the more necessary for me to proceed cautiously from real practice and experience towards a new and different theory of mission.

In any action taken in the name of the church today, one of the key criteria to measure the fitness of what is being done is the bible. "Is it biblical? Is it evangelical? Is it scriptural?" are questions that must be asked time and time again. Could we not, with some value, expose our missionary efforts to this criterion? With all its necessary organization and structure, with all the development entailed in the unfolding history of its successes and failures, the missionary effort should, in its main and basic outlines, be biblical. What would be the result if we were to turn our scriptural spotlight on the work being carried out in the name of mission today, say, in Africa? What would we have to answer if we were asked, "Is the mission work in the church today biblical?"

Of course, the main missionary we see in action in the bible is St. Paul. And we can surely believe that those sections of the Acts and epistles describing the missionary work of this extraordinary man, like the rest of scriptures "were written for our instruction."[1]

St. Paul made three famous missionary journeys, or *safaris,* as we would call them. Before these journeys began, there was no church in the areas under consideration. The three journeys took about ten years in all. They began sometime between 45 and 49 A.D. (probably 47 A.D.) and ended in 57 or 58 A.D.[2]

The first journey of St. Paul, beginning about 47 A.D., took him through the country of Southern Galatia (or the Provinces of Pisidia and Lycaonia).[3] The safari took in about twelve hundred miles in all. The area in which Paul went to preach the gospel was between ten and twenty thousand square miles, depending on how much territory we include in Galatia. There were just three missionaries along on that first journey—Paul, and Barnabas and John Mark. These three missionaries had a territory to evangelize that was the size of a large East African diocese. Paul preached in one place, Lystra for six months[4] and in another, Iconium, for some time,[5] and then left the country, his work finished, the church in the province of South Galatia founded.

The Council of Jerusalem took place after this journey.

The second journey of St. Paul took place between the years of 50–52 A.D. With him on this journey went Silas, Timothy, and Luke, four missionaries in all. This was an even longer safari than the first, perhaps some twenty-six hundred miles. Paul visited the churches he had founded on the first journey, then went on to evangelize areas taking in almost thirty thousand square miles. He went to Macedonia, preached in Thessalonica for five months,[6] in Phillipi for a shorter length of time, then went off to the province of Achaia and labored there for one and a half years[7] at Corinth. He founded the churches in Macedonia and Achaia during the course of this journey and then went back home, his work completed.

The third journey of St. Paul came between the years of 53 and 57 A.D. As many as ten different missionaries are mentioned as taking part in the evangelization of this Roman Province of Asia.[8] He also picked up several workers from the very church he was evangelizing.[9] This was a safari of approximately fourteen hundred miles, and his many efforts were concentrated in a much smaller area, perhaps five thousand square miles in the province of Asia. His main point of attack was Ephesus. He preached the gospel for two and a quarter years,[10] and then left, satisfied that the church was established in the province of Asia.

We have to face the startling fact that before 47 A.D. the church did not exist in these four provinces of the Roman empire. By 57 A.D., a little more than ten years later, due to the missionary work of Paul and a handful of others, the church existed in the provinces of Galatia, Macedonia, Achaia, and Asia. We know these churches from letters afterwards addressed to them as the churches of the Thessalonians, Phillipians, Corinthians, Ephesians, and Galatians.[11]

Not only were the churches established there. St. Paul was satisfied that his work was completed there.

He writes in the year 58 A.D., to the Romans: "All the way from Jerusalem to Illyricum I have preached Christ's good news to the utmost of my capacity" (Rom 15:19). Then a little later on he explains (or complains), "Now, however, having no more work to do here . . . ."[12] And in the same letter he speaks of the churches of Macedonia and Achaia[13] as churches taking in entire provinces.

And all this just shortly after having finished his last missionary journey in the year 57 A.D.

All we can do is look at this and wonder.

What would we find if we applied this biblical criterion to our work today?

We foreign missionaries have been in East Africa for more than a *hundred* years. We started off with two missionaries, like Paul, but when a hundred years had passed we were still here— 1,951 of us, counting only priests, with many generations of our predecessors dead and buried in this land.

Our original safaris from our homeland were much farther than St. Paul's from his, but once arriving at our destination, no single one of us has an area of work to cover anywhere near the staggering areas covered by St. Paul. It would be closer to the truth to say that the areas covered by St. Paul on each journey would closely approximate our present dioceses, in each one of which we have many foreign missionaries, anywhere from twenty to one hundred to a diocese. We won't even mention the means of travel available to Paul and to us.

After one hundred years we still do not consider our work finished. New missionaries are appealed for, for this hundred year old work, and they are still coming.

There is something definitely temporary about Paul's missionary stay in any one place. There is something of a deadly permanence in ours.

Besides the amount of time Paul spent in any one place—two and a half years at Ephesus being the longest stay—there is something else different in Paul's missionary strategy. He evangelized just a few centers in each province (diocesan area today?), and considered his work done.[14] We do not consider our work finished (even apart from the time element involved) until we have fairly inundated a section with missions—placing mission stations a few miles from one another.

We have not even looked at the specific goal Paul had in mind when he was evangelizing a section, nor the method he used, in any detail. We might be even more startled if we did. All we have looked at is his general plan or strategy of missionary work, and that is surprising enough in the light of our own.

We might not agree with St. Paul's general missionary strategy or his overall method. We might give many reasons why his method would not work today, and why the biblical system has evolved into the system we know. At this point I am not really trying to argue against such objections. All I am trying to show is that we must admit what is true.

If we can say nothing else at this point, at least we have to admit that our work, in this respect, is *not* biblical; indeed, we have strayed far from the biblical criterion and method. To doubt this is to deny the staggering amount of evidence in the bible.

When I began to work among the Masai, there were thirty-three thousand Catholic missionary priests in the world, and together with our Protestant brethren and all our missionary predecessors, we could claim to have evangelized eighteen percent of the world. Without trying to disparage the work of obviously sincere men, one could still wish that St. Paul were alive today. Or if this is a futile thought, what about another one: despite all the arguments against it, suppose, instead of the *thirty-three* thousand missionaries of the type we have known, we had *one* thousand men of the mind of Paul, convinced of the method of Paul. I wonder what proportion of the world would be evangelized.

Toward a New Strategy

St. Paul must have had a fair notion of the geography of his known world, judging from the journeys he planned. He must even have had a kind of strategy worked out (like a military campaign), to cover his world.

At least it was a place to begin. What if an attempt was made to follow the lead of St. Paul, the general strategy of St. Paul, on a local level? Wouldn't it change the whole notion of missionary work, the entire method and time needed to carry it out? The idea was intriguing.

Loliondo was the name of the mission to which I was assigned in the diocese of Arusha, in Tanzania, East Africa. It consisted of a mission house for priests, another one for nursing sisters, a small bush hospital, and a little church capable of seating a hundred people. The nearest town, Arusha, was two hundred and fifty difficult miles away. The mission covered an area of five thousand square miles, over which the seminomadic Masai were scattered to the number of approximately thirty thousand inhabitants.

After much scouting and exploring, I discovered that the whole area could be divided into twenty-six sections. A different section could be reached every day if one moved out of the mission house and lived in a Landrover and a tent. Instructions in the Christian message would take about a year in any one section visited once a week. Realistically, six sections could be reached in a year. So, the whole Loliondo area of twenty-six sections could be evangelized in five years; less, if others joined me in the task. This struck me as of extreme importance and significance. It would mean I could leave that particular mission after five years, having completed my work.

Theologically, I considered the fact that Christianity is now a minority religion in the world, and will probably always be so. We should not set out to evangelize everyone, or even the majority of people. We were out to evangelize a minority, but a minority in every section. St. Paul, in his work, evangelized two or three centers in every province, and considered his work done in those provinces. These centers were to become the centers for further evangelization and the spread of the church. It seems he was working on the minority strategy also. My plan would not be to establish two or three centers for the entire area, but a center for every single, individual section of the mission area. That would amount to twenty-six centers, and could actually be considered over-evangelization. Nonetheless, it was a goal to aim at, and it was a radical departure from the current system in that it could actually be finished in five years, whereas the presently existing, static mission of Loliondo had stood there for seven years already with zero results. And the goal envisaged was not to be mission compounds or mission stations in every section, but Christian communities in every section. *Missions* belong to the missionaries. Christian communities belong to the people; indeed, they are the people.

All these practicalities derive from the very important distinction between missionary and pastoral work. Pastoral work, the tending of the Christian flock, by its very nature and definition will never be finished. But the work of evangelization (the biblical definition of missionary work) in any particular area, by its very nature, must be *finishable,* that is, it must be planned and carried out in such a way that it is finishable in the shortest possible time, not in some vague future, but *now.*

Christ's command to evangelize the nations cannot have been directed to a vast, limitless, impossible, insuperable, unfinishable task. St. Paul would never have complained that he had nothing left to do, having finished his task. And in any one area, we can and must finish ours. There are many reasons for believing this to be true. Some have to do with the actual situation of the church in the world, and the distribution of missionary personnel and finances. Others have to do with the attitude of the missionaries themselves who are involved in such a work. Still other reasons stem from the effect produced in the people being evangelized by a prolonged stay of missionaries among them. Finally, there are reasons coming from the actual political and historical situation of today. In many respects we have come to the eleventh hour of the missions.

When I first went to Africa I was assigned to the beautiful country of Kilimanjaro, the twenty thousand foot high mountain on the equator, to learn the Swahili language. I can remember an old missionary telling me that he had spent his life under the snows of Kilimanjaro, and his dream was to die and be buried under the snows of Kilimanjaro. I was deeply impressed at the time. It was a beautiful thought, but looking back on it now I do not think it was a particularly *missionary* thought. Nor are any involving hundred year plans.

NOTES TO CHAPTER 3

1. Roland Allen, *Missionary Methods: St. Paul's or Ours?* (Fleming H. Revell, 1913), p. 4.

2. Alexander Jones, ed., "Introduction to the Letters of St. Paul," *The Jerusalem Bible* (Doubleday and Company, 1966), p. 251.

3. Acts Chap. 13 and 14. Also Jerusalem Bible, p. 251.

4. Acts 14:8–19. Also, Allen, *Missionary Methods,* p. 113.

5. Acts 14:5.

6. Allen, *Missionary Methods,* p. 114.

7. Acts 18:11.

8. Acts 18:18 to 21:17.

9. Acts 19:1–7.

10. Acts 19:9,10.

11. Jerusalem Bible, pp. 255–263. Also, Allen, *Missionary Methods,* p. 3.

12. Rom 15:23.

13. Rom 15:26.

14. Allen, *Missionary Methods,* p. 19.

4

A Time to Speak and a Time to Act

The Unknown God

The old Masai chief, Ndangoya, in calling together the people of his own and neighboring kraals represented the first community of Masai, the first section of the mission area, to be evangelized. There were five other communities, located in five other different sections of the mission, that, together with Ndangoya's community, constituted the first step in bringing the gospel to the Masai. Going back and forth among these pagan communities week by week, I soon realized that not one week would go by without some surprising rejoinder or reaction or revelation from these Masai. My education was beginning in earnest.

The process followed was simple. I would mention a religious theme or thought and ask to hear their opinion on it, and then I would tell them what I believed on the same subject, a belief I had come eight thousand miles to share with them. I have done pastoral and social work in America and Africa, and have taught in a major seminary. But I have never been so tested in my life as by these pagan sons and daughters of the plains. I soon began to realize that I was involved in a basic confrontation, the most ultimate confrontation Christianity can ever have—the one with paganism, with the world that does not believe as we believe.

I remember the very first week of instructions when I asked the Masai to tell me what they thought about God. I was more than startled when a young Masai elder stood up and said, "If I ever run into God, I will put a spear through him."

Here he was immersed on one side in an unshakable belief in the existence of God, and faced on the other with the numbing reality of a life that includes pain and sickness, death of children and loss of cattle. This young elder was trying to come to terms with a God who seemed to be responsible for it all. His thoughts were really not very far removed from those of many young Americans and Europeans today; not really very different from the mentality of Albert Camus in *The Plague*. This is the point at which religious reflection began for him in a very real way. So this is the point at which we began to speak with him and his fellow tribesmen about the Christian idea of God. The question evoked by this comment of his was *his* question, not ours, and we tried to answer it the best we could.

It is as good a starting place as any for preaching the gospel to the Masai.

For the Masai, there is only one God, *Engai*, but he goes by many names. Sometimes they call him *male*, sometimes *female*. When he is kind and propitious they call him the black God. When he is angry, the red God. Sometimes they call him rain, since this is a particularly pleasing manifestation of God. But he is always the one, true God. They asked if we did the same. I had to admit that for us, also, God goes by many names, and that in the long history of the bible, the same is true. Indeed, I was to find from research, as a result of this question of theirs, that the Jews called God, on occasion, fire, breeze and God of the mountain.[1] They were a bit incredulous to learn, that, for all practical purposes, we leave the female out of God, and we consider him as only male, which is, of course, as patently wrong as considering God only female. God is neither male nor female, which is an animal classification, but certainly embodies the qualities which we like to believe exist in both. If the Masai wanted to refer to God as she as well as he, I could certainly find nothing theologically incorrect about the notion. Their idea seems much more embracing and universal than ours—and not a whit less biblical:

"Does a woman forget her baby at the breast, or fail to cherish the son of her womb? Yet even if these forget, I will never forget you" (Is 49:15).

Then they told me of God, Engai, who loved rich people more than poor people, healthy people more than the sick, the God who loved good people because they were good, and rewarded them for their goodness. They told me of God who hated evil people—"those dark, evil ones out there"—and punished them for their evil. Then they told me of the God who loved the Masai more than all the other tribes, loved them fiercely, jealously, exclusively. His power was known throughout the lush grasslands of the Masai steppes; his protection saved them from all the surrounding, hostile, Masai-hating tribes, and assured them of victory in war over these tribes; his goodness was seen in the water and rain and cattle and children he gave them.

I finally spoke up and told them they reminded me of another great people that lived long ago, and live until the present time. "They are the Hebrew tribe, the Jews, the Israelis. They are famous the world over for having preserved in the world the knowledge of the one, true God. But it was not always easy for them. They often tried to restrict that God to their tribe and to their land, and so made him less of a God than he really was.

"One time, in the early days of their tribe, he called a man named Abraham and said to him, Abraham, come away from this land of yours. Leave your people and your tribe and your land, and come to the land I will show you. And all nations will be blessed in you, if you do this.

"The God of the tribe of Abraham had become a God who was no longer free. He was trapped in that land, among that tribe. He had to be freed from that nation, that tribe, that land in order to become the High God."

I realized when I reached this crucial point that I was touching a sensitive nerve of the Masai.

Paul Tillich points out that only if God is exclusively God, unconditioned and unlimited by anything other than himself, is there a true monotheism, and only then is the power over space and time broken.[2] He lists as examples of limiting spatial concepts such things as blood, race, clan, tribe, and family. Abraham's call was the turning point. It was the beginning of the end for polytheism. God must be separated from his nation to become the High God.[3]

Each African tribe believes in God, and it is generally considered to be a monotheistic God. But each tribe likes to restrict the attention and protection of this God to its own territory, thus planting the seeds for polytheism.

I continued talking with the people who were now listening very closely: "When Abraham followed God out of his land, there began on this earth the story of the one, true, living, High God.

"Everyone knows how devout you Masai are, the faith you have, your beautiful worship of God. You have known God and he has loved you. But I wonder if, perhaps, you have not become like the people of the tribe of Abraham. Perhaps God has become trapped in this Masai country, among this tribe. Perhaps God is no longer free here. What will the Kikuyu do to protect themselves against this God of the Masai—and the Sonjo? They will have to have their own gods. Perhaps the story of Abraham speaks also to you. Perhaps you Masai also must leave your nation and your tribe and your land, at least in your thoughts, and go in search of the High God, the God of all tribes, the God of the world. Perhaps your God is not free. Do not try to hold him here or you will never know him. Free your God to become the High God. You have known this God and worshiped him, but he is greater than you have known. He is the God not only of the Masai, but also my God, and the God of the Kikuyu and Sonjo, and the God of every tribe and nation in the world.

"And the God who loves rich people and hates poor people? The God who loves good people and hates evil people—'those dark, evil ones out there'? The God who loves us because we are good and hates us because we are evil? There is no God like that. There is only the God who loves us no matter how good or how evil we are, the God you have worshiped without really knowing him, the truly unknown God—the High God."

There was silence. Perhaps I had gone too far. The mention

of a wandering search that took a lifetime must have evoked memories of their own ancestors recalled from generation to generation around nomadic campfires. Abraham himself must have seemed like a long lost ancestor to them, he who used to like to "fill his eyes with cattle." The Masai are a Nilotic people, and they have a dim remembrance of their ancestors crossing the "great river" in their wandering exile. If you look at a map of Northeastern Africa you will find the record of that historic trek. All along the way the sites they passed through have Masai names until today. The word *khartoum* in the Masai language means "we have acquired." That is where they believed they acquired their first cattle. Khartoum today is the capital of the Sudan. When they came up out of the steamy jungles of the Sudan into the cold plains of Kenya, they said, "nairobi," which means cold, and it stands as the main city in Kenya and East Africa today. They finally discovered their promised land of milk and honey (the two most desired and appreciated items in the Masai diet) in the empire they carved out of East Africa. But the High God! That was something else.

Finally someone broke the silence with a question. Whether he asked the question out of curiosity or anger, I do not know. I only know it surprised me:

"This story of Abraham—does it speak only to the Masai? Or does it speak also to you? Has your tribe found the High God? Have you known him?"

I was about to give a glib answer, when all of a sudden I thought of Joan of Arc. I don't know why I thought of her, but suddenly I remembered that since the time of Jeanne D'Arc, if not before, the French have conceived of God (*le bon Dieu*—what would the Masai think of him?) as being rather exclusively and intimately associated with their quest for glory. I wonder what god they prayed to?

Americans have some kind of certainty that "almighty God" will always bless *their* side in all their wars. Hitler never failed to call on the help of *"Gott, der Allmächtige"* in all his speeches, in all his adventures. A Nazi doctor once told me that they could always count on the Catholic school children to pray for Hitler every morning, to ask God's blessing on him. What god, the Teuton god?

I have been to many parishes in America where they prayed for victory in war. I recognized the god they were praying to—the tribal god. I will recognize him more easily now, after having lived among the Masai. And what about the God who loves good people, industrious people, clean people, rich people, and punishes bad people, lazy people, dirty people, thieving people, people without jobs and on welfare—"those dark, evil people out there?" Which god is that?

I sat there for a long time in silence looking at the Masai people. They called their God Engai. Well, that is no more strange-sounding than our gods. The god invoked by the pope to bless the troops of Mussolini about to embark on the plunder of Ethiopia, and the god invoked by an American cardinal to bless the "soldiers of Christ" in Vietnam, and the god of French glory, and the German god of Hitler were no more the High God of scripture than is "Diana of the Ephesians" or Engai of the Masai of East Africa.

To each one of these cultures must ever be presented again the proclamation of the message, symbolized in the call of Abraham—to leave their land and their nation, to learn of the High God, the God of the world. *All* nations are to be blessed in Abraham.

I finally spoke out again, and I marveled at how small my voice sounded. I said something I had no intention of saying when I had come to speak to the Masai that morning:

"No, *we have not* found the High God. My tribe has not known him. For us, too, he is the unknown God. But we are searching for him. I have come a long, long distance to invite you to search for him with us. Let us search for him together. Maybe, together, we will find him."

I got up and walked away from the Masai village, to go back to my tent. As I walked, I remembered the shortest summation of the gospel message St. Paul ever made, in his letter to Titus (3:4): "The goodness and kindness of God our Savior has appeared to all men." That is really what I had been trying to say. I hoped I had gotten it across, at least to my friend, the young Masai elder who wanted to put a spear through God.

I walked away numb from my first confrontation with paganism.

As far as preaching the gospel to the Masai was concerned, a greater obstacle to it than the God who stood in danger of being speared, was the God who in no way could be speared, or even touched—so remote was he. I once asked a Masai elder where God lived, and he took me away from the village and the trees so that I could get a clear view of the sky. He then pointed past the fleeting, fleecy white clouds, beyond the pale blue dome of the sky to a patch of dark blue, deep, deep in the sky. In his astronomical view, admittedly limited, he was pointing to the farthest point away from the place where we were standing. "Engai lives there," he said. A terribly remote God.

Not a God of creation who exists in and with the things he brought into being. Creation is a key part of revelation. No nation, no culture could have come to it on its own. For the cultures outside of Christianity, the earth is complete once and for all, and the world is not going anywhere in particular; everything is chaotic and directionless. People of those cultures are trapped in the terrible dilemma of a fatalistic world vision—empty of the notion of continuing creation and personal responsibility and opportunity. A missionary's greatest contribution to the people for whom he works might well be to separate them from God, free them from their idea of God.

No nation, no culture on earth could ever have come to the notion of continuing creation. It is probably at this point we begin to realize that revelation, as it comes to us—the gospel, the secret hidden from the beginning of the world—is outside every culture, is supracultural. It comes from outside our cultures and yet is destined for all of them—a supracultural, unchanging message of good news.

The Judaeo-Christian religious inheritance has never dismissed as illusion what comes from the hand of God. The world is Maya, illusion, in the Hindu culture, an illusion to be cast off in reaching the state of perfection. That might be very inspiring and uplifting, but it does not really offer much hope to a world of flesh and blood, of poverty and hunger. It is only in the Jewish and Christian faith that a Messianic hope first breaks upon mankind.[4] The lack of a future tense in the Masai language is, I believe, symptomatic of a lack of expectant hope for the future. I doubt if it is possible for any pagan culture to take part in true human development.

*   *   *   *

One time after I had finished a year of instructions in one of my villages, a lady resident of the village said to me: "I think I understand what your message (the gospel) is saying to us. You are telling us that we must love the people of Kisangiro. Why must we do that?"

Kisangiro happened to be the next village, three miles away. The people of that village were of the same tribe as the people of her village, but of a different clan. Being people who existed beyond the boundaries of the clan, they qualified for her as being "those dark, evil people out there." This young lady's difficulty lay in extending the obligation of love not to me and my white-faced tribe, or to the brown-faced Indian traders, or to people of hostile, alien tribes surrounding her own. Her difficulty lay within her own tribe, towards people of another clan who lived three miles down the road. That was the giant step for her. That was the chasm impossible to cross. That was the testing point of Christianity.

Can you imagine speaking with this lady about nation building, or about joining in a common endeavor to establish a school or medical center for the surrounding villages, or about a joint effort to build a road between her village and the hated and feared village of Kisangiro?

If someone does not help that village lady, and millions like her, through that first step, across that impassable chasm; if she and they do not come to believe in a God above all the tribes and clans, and in a sacred world of unlimited possibilities and expectant hope, there will be no nation building, no human development. And she and her fellow Africans could well be destroyed by the development and science and technology we bring to them so enthusiastically.

The Nations

Masai country in present-day Tanzania is an isolated place. I would be reminded of this sitting in my tent each night, alone from seven o'clock onward, the Masai village near which I was camped, completely closed in by a circular, thorn barrier fence, against the wild animals in the midst of which these people lived, against the evil spirits of whom they were terrified, against the night. There were no lights, no artificial sounds coming from modern technology, no sounds of traffic, no refrigerators humming or air conditioners whirring, no amplified rock beat, no blare of radio or T.V. The only sounds I would ever hear night after night were natural ones, the wind rushing across the plains, the rain drumming on the tent and splashing on the ground outside, the campfire crackling, an occasional roar or grunt from a lion. Sometimes I would see the yellow eyes of the lions as I replenished the fire. They seemed to be drawn to the fire, checking out who had invaded their turf. Sometimes I would see them in the dawn going back from the kill, or a lonely leopard with his evil eyes watching me drive past in the early morning light.

The extreme isolation, the solitude, cannot help but get to you, do strange things to you. You begin to wonder if there is really a world outside, or if it is something you only dreamed up. You question whether the world is not passing you by. Occasionally in the night you see the satellites sent up from another continent passing silently through the African, equatorial sky. While your fellow countrymen are hurling themselves at the stars and stepping on the moon, you are in the midst of people from the same planet in the same century who have to barricade themselves in, away from wild animals and evil spirits.

It makes you wonder when you come face to face with these people on the morrow if anything you do or say in such isolation can be relevant to the real world; if anything you decide to discuss about religion would necessarily be so insular and provincial that it could have little meaning to the rest of the world. Yet, at times, sitting there by the morning fire in the cold Masai highlands, I could sense that what these people were pondering, many had pondered before them. They were touching the raw nerve of a sore that is festering throughout the world. They were reflecting on the possibility of opening themselves up to every other tribe and race on the face of the earth, bringing with them all the cultural and spiritual riches of their tribe, exposing themselves at the same time to every sort of exploitation and waste.

If the God of the world were the God of all the tribes and nations of the world, and loved them all equally, that would change things, as far as the way they looked at other tribes and clans, and acted towards them. The Masai had become great by the conquest of most of the tribes that had come across their path. Like the lion, whose grunt they imitated in their dances, they walked proud and unafraid across the plains. Must they now bleat like sheep, timid, stupid, prone to being lost and slaughtered?

I do not know if the reader can appreciate the novelty and difficulty of such a thought for them. We can glibly say the human race is one; we all belong to a brotherhood, all sons and daughters of a common Father, all equal in value and importance. We have inherited such a thought. I doubt if we could have ever come to it on our own. It was an essential part of the gospel message, with which Paul and the early evangelists turned the world upside down.

Suppose you belonged to a tribe like the Masai, for whom there was no abstract notion of brotherhood, but only a concrete, specific idea of brotherhood, arrived at by initiation and extending only to a restricted group within a clan line—an age-group brotherhood called *orporor*. It was by no means universal. It was limited to those initiated within a certain time span, generally a seven year period. This orporor taught them everything they knew of love and loyalty and dedication and responsibility and sacrifice. But it was necessarily limited by that very time, that very space.

What was being suggested to them in place of this limited and specific brotherhood, was so disturbing as to be frightening, so beautiful as to be tantalizing.

The use of the word "brother" by the black race in America as a specific greeting and designation, is amazingly similar in its implications and in its limitations.

One morning while the old man, Ndangoya, and his community were struggling with this problem, I could not help but notice a colleague of his, a man named Keriko, in obvious pain. I was certain he was ill. But my Masai catechist helper, Paul, chuckled at my concern.

"Are you worried about old man Keriko? Don't worry, he is all right. You see, for a Masai there is not much need to think in life. Almost everything he learns, he learns by memory, by rote. It becomes automatic for him, like tying your shoes or buttoning your shirt is for you. He learns about food and clothes and houses and kraals and cattle and grasses and women by memory—even things about God and religion. When he needs an answer to a question, all he has to do is reach into his memory and come up with the correct answer. He can reach his adulthood without thinking at all. What you are asking Keriko to do is

to take the first thought about the Masai brotherhood of the
orporor, and the second thought about the human race and the
God of all the tribes, and to put the two thoughts together to
make a new thought. That is very difficult work. What you are
witnessing in Keriko is the pain on the face of a man who is
thinking for the first time in his life." Paul chuckled again out
loud. He had a unique sense of humor.

What the Masai were wrestling with was a decision and a dilemma, in miniature, that the whole world is facing, and has
faced many times before.

Before I came to Masailand, or even to Africa, I used to wonder, whenever I came across it, at the insistence the bible, especially the New Testament, placed on the *nations,* on the drive
towards the *nations.* I used to wonder if this was not, perhaps, an
obsession of classical times, that had little meaning for today, for
us. It is only since I came to Africa, that I have seen how wrong I
was.

The burning hatred, hostility, and prejudice of one race or
tribe toward another is the force that has torn apart the Congo
and Nigeria since I came to Africa, seared Rhodesia, and is
building up to an explosion in South Africa. It is the force boil-
ing over in the Middle East between Arab and Jew, in the Far
East between China and Russia, and in America between black
and white. It is the same force that Paul and Peter had to fight
against so desperately. The whole bible squared off against this
elementary evil.

To fail to see this in the New Testament is to miss indeed the
main thrust of the gospel message—the universalism of the
good news. So many people today are asking if missionaries are
important or even necessary. I would have to answer: "Yes they
are, perhaps more for this reason than for anything else." Every
artificial attempt from the time of the Tower of Babel, up to the
United Nations to "make a great people, a people which is one,"
has failed. I believe that only Christianity has the inherent capa-

bility to accomplish this, the inner strength necessary to match the primeval force of racism and tribalism.

For this reason, more than any other, do the final words of our Lord make any sense at all to me, "Go out to the ends of the earth and preach the gospel to every nation."

The irony in this particular case of the African Masai, who know little, if anything, about the long history of the church, is that history is now on their side. The christianized Jews and the citizens of the Roman empire have been shoved aside in Christian history. Now it is the turn of the European-Americans to be passed over. Before this century is out, even as the Christian church continues on its way as a dwindling minority in the world, in this same period, the members of the predominantly nonwhite third world, for the first time in history, will begin to become the majority in the Christian church.[5]

As I pass on this message of Peter and Paul and John to the segment of a nation before me, I am overcome with a kind of melancholy. History is playing itself out, in capsule form, before my very eyes. As I watch these Masai men and women, the old man Ndangoya, the agonizing Keriko, and their community, ponder the implications of this message, I know they will have to work out their own response to it. And their response, whatever it is, will not have very much to do with me.

As the message passes from us to them, I find myself hoping that they will make better use of it than we did.

Sin, Salvation, and Culture Blindness

Going back to visit and speak with Ndangoya and his friends and the people of the other villages week after week, we necessarily had to come into conflict, not with them, but with the church that sent us. There were several things wrong with the neat format our church and its theologians had set up for us.

One thing was that we were sent out as church-planters, church-builders. For all practical purposes we were sent out to preach not Christianity, but the church. The church was the Ark of salvation. Those inside the ark were saved. Those outside perished. This was an unanalyzed assumption on which all missionary work was built. According to this assumption, we were to consider the Masai a lost people, and therefore had to convert as many of them as possible by converting them in great numbers. That would, of course, imply that all the Masai who died before we got there were lost. Perhaps if we lived in Europe or America and knew of the Masai only theoretically, we might have been tempted to come to such an unhappy conclusion. But living as we do among the Masai, and knowing them and their lives, and being friends with them, we have an advantage over the theologians and theoreticians of Europe and America, who study a pagan people and a pagan religion at a distance.

Salvation is not a magic formula produced by a secret mixture of sacraments and church membership. It is the result of love of God and grace and holiness and goodness. It is all one process, continuous, unbroken. Goodness and holiness are the beginning of salvation, and they do not reside exclusively in Europe and America. I have seen too many good and holy pagans in Africa to believe that. The Masai are no more a lost people than the Christians of Africa, or of Europe and America, are. The Masai are a people loved by God, and the signs of this love are manifest in their lives. Salvation is as possible for them as it is for us. Making salvation possible or easier for the Masai could not be our reason for bringing Christianity to them. If I had been inclined to think it was our reason, I would soon have been disabused of the notion by the old man, Ndangoya, who one day told me, "This High God of whom you speak, he could not possibly love Christians more than pagans, could he? Or he would be more of a tribal god than ours."

Another assumption we had to discard in going to the Masai was the very assumption that had kept us from evangelizing them in the first place, an assumption and declaration we had heard on every side: "It is impossible to preach the gospel directly to the Masai."

I believe such an opinion stems from that "lost tribe" mentality, or from the conviction that the pagan peoples of the earth are not quite bright enough, or open enough, or good enough to accept Christianity directly, if it is presented to them, but must somehow be lured into Christianity.

It is on such a nebulous and uncertain foundation that the entire structure of what has come to be called preevangelization rests. Preevangelization is a noble theory constructed by theologions, according to which it is stated that not all peoples are ready for the gospel, and somehow must be made ready for it. In its arrogant cultural assumption, preevangelization may be the most vicious system of thought and action ever invented by missiological theologians.

It smacks mightily of the attitude of Dr. Livingstone—who, in the last century strode into the universities of Europe making a plea to the young people of those universities to come to Africa to help him make the Africans "free, civilized, and Christian"— in that order. He had an incredibly high and naive idea of Christendom.

Are the pagans of today, like the Masai for instance, somehow in a more desperate antigospel situation than the pagans of classical times. Are the Africans pagans of today living in a more sin-filled, grace-less atmosphere? The apostles came in contact with a world which was unconscious of the niceties of what we call sexual morality. Read closely the epistles of St. Paul: for instance, the one to the Ephesians, where he mentions the actual situation of his world. Pagan worship and pagan theater were often starkly sexual. Among the Phyrigions whom Paul evangelized on his first missionary journey, and from whom he made his first converts, marriage was unknown.[6]

Are Masai pagans further away from salvation than European and American Christians? Is endemic and incurable cattle thiev-

ing further removed from salvation than assassinating and killing and selling deadly weapons and cheating in business and
lying in advertising?

As far as the Masai were concerned, we had to overthrow the
assumption that they were not yet ready for the gospel. We had
to believe that the gospel, the message of Christianity, the revelation of God to man, is for everyone, for the entire human race,
for every people in every segment of that human race—as they
are, where they are, now. Or else we would have to retranslate
the mission mandate to: "Preach the gospel to all the nations—
except to those who are not ready."

Another assumption on which missionary work was built was
this: we had to convince the world of sin, instead of leaving that
task to the Holy Spirit, as Christ suggested. We had to convince
the world of sin, or the world would never feel the need for
redemption, and the Redeemer. We had to tell them of the sin of
Adam, original sin, which we all inherited, or they would never
feel any need for Christ. It was the assumption underlying all
missionary catechesis. This way we could lead them to Christ.

Having no other tradition to rely on, I did just that with the
Masai—the story of Adam and Eve and the garden and the fruit
tree, and the serpent and the Fall.

The trouble was that they had their own stories about the
beginning of the human race. And in their stories, as in the
stories of every pagan tribe with which I am acquainted, there is
the recounting of a Fall. In no way do any of the stories bring
about a consciousness of guilt, or need for personal redemption,
any more, I suspect, than the story of Adam succeeds in doing
for the young people of our culture today.

The Masai complained, with some justification, that our story
about the beginning of the human race is more than a bit ag-
riculturally biased, what with the garden and the fruit trees and
the command to till the soil. For them, the cowboys of East
Africa, tilling the soil is anathema. Only an *olmeg* (a farmer, a

barbarian) would cut open the thin layer of topsoil nurturing the life-giving grass of the Masai steppes, exposing it to the merciless equatorial sun, and turning it into desert within years. So, understandably, all their stories of the beginning of the human race are veterinary in character, that is, they all refer to cattle raising in some way.

The story of the garden of Eden was bad enough. I followed with a worse one, the story of the first farmer, Cain, murdering the first cattlemen, Abel—the beginning, as the Masai saw it even by our accounting, of all the troubles between the two groups even until now. And Cain got away with it, just as the farmers do today, and always have, with the government backing them. They began to wonder if that book I held in my hands with such great reverence, was not some kind of an agricultural or governmental plot against them.

And after hearing their myths and stories, it seemed a little strange offering ours about a man and woman in the garden of Eden, and a fruit tree with forbidden fruit, as the definitive and final story about the origin of evil in the world, pretending our story were not a myth, a myth with a very important teaching perhaps, but a myth nonetheless, and one encased in a very pronounced cultural setting at that. I never told the story again.

So I had to try in other ways to convince them of sin. I had nothing else to go by, except the theology I had studied, to set the stage for the need of redemption, of Christ. The missionaries of Hawaii must have been tortured by the same thought. We and they had somehow become convinced that selling guilt was indeed our mission.

After I had worked along this line for some time, I became conscious of the hopelessness I was engendering in them by building my teaching on the foundation stone of sin. I was haunted by the look in the eyes of these good pagan people as I went on insisting they were steeped in sin, and their peers, who had not even heard the word I was bringing, even more so. And their ancestors, whom they did not worship as existing spirits, but whom they revered as founders of their tribe and doers of great deeds, were they all a sinful, wicked people?

The Masai consider their ancestors and their peers beautiful. How can it be a part of the Christian message to tell them they are not? And if you look honestly and openly at pagans—as almost every missionary can testify—they *are* beautiful people. St. Paul and St. Peter said as much: "The loving kindness of God has appeared to all men . . . . God lets each nation (each tribe, each culture) go its own way . . . . He is evident to them in the happiness he gives them."

There is no use arguing that it isn't true happiness they have, or that they aren't really happy—because they *are,* at least in that momentary escape from their loneliness and hopelessness while drinking the rich butterfat milk of their Zebu cattle, or striding across the Masai plains, or dancing the beautiful dances of nomads. St. Paul says this happiness is a sign of God among them. He was there before we ever got there. It is simply up to us to bring him out so they recognize him.

While I was going about the evangelizing of these first villages, I noticed from time to time, a man on the outskirts of the different communities under instruction, the same man appearing in different places. He seemed poorer than the average Masai, and he did not seem to belong to any of the communities. One day in the midst of our discussion, he asked a question. It was a simple question but it mystified me. He asked, "Can you people bring forgiveness of sin?"

I hadn't gotten around to forgiveness yet (or confession). I was still trying to get across the consciousness and reality of sin. I thought the man was really not paying attention. I did not answer his question. I told him I would get to that some other day. Then, afterwards, I found out who he was. He was a man who had committed a great sin against the taboos of the Masai tribe. So he had become an outcast, belonging to no community. No community wanted him or was willing to have him live and work with them. A man with a sin on his head would bring nothing but evil on any community with which he lived. The worst part of it was that the sin in question was unforgivable. There was no forgiveness possible from God or man. He was destined to live the rest of his life as a despicable outcast. No wonder he asked me if I and my people could bring forgiveness. By the time I had found out about all of this he was gone. I felt miserable.

That man and his people knew all about sin. What they did not know about was forgiveness of sin. They did not even know it was possible.

I found out more about sin and the Masai. Some sins were unforgivable, like that man's sin. Other sins were not unforgivable, but nearly so. The difficulty involved in obtaining forgiveness for certain sins was so great that it bordered on impossibility. The Masai had to sweat and strain and suffer to reach forgiveness, even when it was possible.

If a son offended his father seriously, this was considered a sin of great magnitude. The sin not only brought a disruption in the relationship between the father and the son, but in the whole community and village where they lived. The son was banished from the community and was even shunned by his colleagues in the military encampments in which they were required to spend time as warriors. It was thought that a kind of curse followed a "sinful" person around, and brought misfortune on all who associated with him. This state of affairs could go on for months or years or even a lifetime.

Sometimes the peers of the father would encourage him to ask God for the "spittle of forgiveness" so that he could forgive his son and bring blessing once again on the village. Spittle, a very sacred element of a living, breathing human, was considered the sign of forgiveness. It was not *just* a sign, as we might be inclined to describe it, or an empty sign bereft of meaning. It was an African sign, which means it was a symbolism in which the sign is as real as the thing it signifies. (We might call it an *effective* sign, one in which the sign effects what it signifies. We could even call it a sacrament.) In other words, spittle was not just a sign of forgiveness. It *was* forgiveness. And so the father prayed to God for that spittle. Sometimes it was not granted him. He could spend the night on a mountainside praying for it. I once visited an old man doing just that. I sat with him in the middle of the night as he prayed in vain for the spittle of forgiveness.

Sometimes it is given him. Whenever it is, word is sent immediately out to the bush to the guilty son. During that same period that son might have been advised time and time again by his own peers to return and ask forgiveness of his father. But as with young people anywhere in the world, that can be a very onerous and distasteful task. But if word does come that the spittle of forgiveness has been granted his father, he will be earnestly entreated by his peers to take advantage of it. They will accompany him back to the village. And his father will be waiting with other elders. The two groups will cross from different sides of the village towards each other in the center. When they arrive there together, the son will ask his father's forgiveness, and the father will spit on him, and forgiveness comes, and there is great rejoicing.

I came across another extraordinary custom of the Masai. Sometimes the sin occurs, not between individuals, but among groups in the same community. One family might offend another family, and disruption sets in on the whole community. This can be disastrous to a nomadic type community who must have unity above all else for the sake of their herding together and moving together and for their common defense against enemies. A disruption like this can rupture the whole agreement or pact or covenant on which the community first came together and on which it remains together. If at all possible, both the offending and the offended family must be brought back together by an act of forgiveness sought and bestowed. So at the behest of the total community both families prepare food. The word for food in Masai is *endaa*. But this will be a special kind of food called the *endaa sinyati*, meaning *holy food*. This holy food is brought to the center of the village by the two families accompanied by the rest of the community, encouraging both families all along the way. There in the center of the village the food is exchanged between the two families, each family accepting the food prepared by the other family. Then the holy food is eaten by both families, and when it is, forgiveness comes, and the people say that a new *osotua* has begun. *Osotua* is the word for covenant or pact or testament.

A new testament of forgiveness is brought about by the exchange of holy food. What can one say?

The Lion Is God

This mighty struggle and effort of pagans to reach forgiveness touched me very deeply. It sent me back to the sources of Christianity to begin again to try to find out what it was all about. I went back to the New Testament, to the Acts and the epistles, to Peter and Paul, who were the first ones to preach the gospel to a pagan world. What does it mean to preach the Christian gospel to such a world?

If you study the apostolic approach very closely, you will see that something is missing. Sin is missing. There is no mention of original sin or any other kind of sin. Sin will come in later, *after Christ,* after getting to know Christ, in relation to Christ, but the sin portrayed by the first preachers of the Christian gospel is forgiven sin, something entirely different—the *felix culpa.* After all, isn't that the only kind of sin there is in the world, forgiven sin?

Christ, after his resurrection, said the same thing: "Now that the resurrection is a reality, now that forgiveness of sins is accomplished in this new covenant, go out to all the earth and preach the good news of the forgiveness of sins to all the nations." Isn't that what he is recorded as saying in Luke and elsewhere?

This *is* good news, to the Masai, to the guilty man cast out of his community, to the sinful son and to the offending family. I do not have to convince them of sin. They know of sin. What they did not know of was forgiveness. It has touched the earth. This is where Christianity parts company from Judaism and from Hinduism and from paganism. Sin is a conquered thing. This is a redeemed world. One wonders if one should dare talk to pagans about sin—apart from Christ, until they know Christ.

The job of a missionary, after all, is not to teach sin, but rather the forgiveness of sin.

It is all clear to me now, many years later. It was not clear to me when I first began to evangelize the Masai. Whereas, at that time, I felt I had got off to a fairly good start as far as God and creation were concerned, I truly bogged down when I came to man and salvation and sin. The nearest colleague with whom I could confer on such a matter was two hundred and fifty miles away. I had to face the difficulty alone and it almost finished me. I became discouraged in a way it would be hard to describe. More than that, before I began to see the way out of the mire, I was ready to give up. I was ready to announce to the church that had sent me, and to anyone else who wanted to listen, that Christianity was not valid—not valid for these Masai, perhaps not valid even for me. I suppose you would call it a crisis of faith, a loss of faith. I had begun to doubt the very message of Christianity.

I can sympathize with and feel with young Americans, whom I have met, who are going through the agony of unbelief. I used to think that faith was a head trip, a kind of intellectual assent to the truths and doctrines of our religion. I know better now. When my faith began to be shattered, I did not hurt in my head. I hurt all over.

Months later when all this had passed, I was sitting talking with a Masai elder about the agony of belief and unbelief. He used two languages to respond to me—his own and Kiswahili. He pointed out that the word my Masai catechist, Paul, and I had used to convey *faith* was not a very satisfactory word in their language. It meant literally *"to agree to."* I, myself, knew the word had that shortcoming. He said "to believe" like that was similar to a white hunter shooting an animal with his gun from a great distance. Only his eyes and his fingers took part in the act. We should find another word. He said for a man really to believe is like a lion going after its prey. His nose and eyes and ears pick up the prey. His legs give him the speed to catch it. All the power of his body is involved in the terrible death leap and single blow to the neck with the front paw, the blow that actually kills. And as the animal goes down the lion envelops it in his arms (Africans refer to the front legs of an animal as its arms) pulls it to himself, and makes it part of himself. This is the way a lion kills. This is the way a man believes. This is what faith is.

I looked at the elder in silence and amazement. Faith understood like that would explain why, when my own was gone, I ached in every fiber of my being. But my wise old teacher was not finished yet.

"We did not search you out, Padri," he said to me. "We did not even want you to come to us. You searched us out. You followed us away from your house into the bush, into the plains, into the steppes where our cattle are, into the hills where we take our cattle for water, into our villages, into our homes. You told us of the High God, how we must search for him, even leave our land and our people to find him. But we have not done this. We have not left our land. We have not searched for him. He has searched for us. He has searched *us* out and found us. All the time we think we are the lion. In the end, the lion is God."

The lion is God. Of course. Goodness and kindness and holiness and grace and divine presence and creating power and salvation were here before I got here. Even the fuller understanding of God's revelation to man, of the gospel, of the salvific act that had been accomplished once and for all for the human race was here before I got here. My role as a herald of that gospel, as a messenger of the news of what had already happened in the world, as the person whose task it was to point to "the one who had stood in their midst whom they did not recognize" was only a small part of the mission of God to the world. It was a mysterious part, a part barely understood. It was a necessary part, a demanded part—"Woe to me if I do not preach the gospel." It was a role that would require every talent and insight and skill and gift and strength I had, to be spent without question, without stint, and yet in the humbling knowledge that only that part of it would be made use of which fit into the immeasurably greater plan of the relentless, pursuing God whose will on the world not be thwarted. The lion is God.

It was going to be a decidedly difficult task, bringing the Christian gospel of forgiveness, and the Christian understanding of salvation to a culture so different from my own, a task calling for extreme care and delicate caution and much humility. So many mistakes could be made. Americans can sometimes be victims of the most incredible culture blindness. I should know. I am one of them.

NOTES TO CHAPTER 4

1. Ex 20:18; 1 Kings 19:12; Ex 6:3.
2. Paul Tillich, *Theology of Culture* (Oxford University Press, 1964), p. 32.
3. Ibid. p. 35.
4. Barbara Ward, *The Rich Nations and the Poor Nations* (W. W. Norton and Co., 1962), p. 21.
5. David B. Barrett, "AD 2000: 350 Million Christians in Africa," *International Review of Mission* 59, No. 233 (Jan. 1970).
6. Roland Allen, *Missionary Methods: St. Paul's or Ours?* (Fleming H. Revell), pp. 43, 51.

5

What Do You Think of the Christ?

The Man Jesus

Once when I was home on leave, I was giving a talk to seniors in an American Catholic high school. When I had finished, a girl stood up with her eyes flashing and, with evident hostility in her voice, said to me, "You speak so warmly of Jesus Christ. Well, Mahatma Gandhi I can take. Buddha, and even Mohammed I can take. But this 'Christ Cat' I cannot take."

All the others in the room, including myself, were a little taken back by the vehemence of her remark. I really do not know what occasioned it in her life. I never found out. But I did find out that, although no one else in the class had the same antagonism towards Jesus that she did, no one else in the class believed in Christ the way Christians normally do. No one there believed in the resurrection of Christ or in the eucharist. Several seniors, in continuing the discussion, referred to Christ as "that deity up there." Some asked why we really need "another deity" like Jesus. One questioned why we couldn't have a Christianity without Christ. It was just one small class of seniors in one American high school, but it did represent twelve years of Catholic teaching and Christian instruction.

I often wondered afterwards about those young people. I wondered if they had ever been exposed to Jesus Christ and the gospel. I wondered, too, why they kept referring to him as "that deity." It is a curious way, to say the least, to describe Jesus of Nazareth. I wondered if it was the initial image they had of him—"that deity."

Most of the Masai that I got to know in Africa had never heard of Jesus, did not even know his name. Some, who had contact with the outside world, had heard his name, at least as it was contained in the title given to those people of other tribes, whom they met, who called themselves "Christ people," or Christians. There was just the slightest ring of superiority and arrogance in the title. But the farther afield I went from the mission of Loliondo during those days of evangelization, the fewer people I met who knew the name, Jesus Christ. Today, years later, there are many more who know his name, but when they speak of him, whether in conversation or teaching or prayer, I do not think they ever refer to him as the deity, Jesus. They prefer the name "oltung'ani Yesu," which would be translated—"the man Jesus." Even in their Creed they speak of him as the "oltung'ani Yesu."

It is important to them that he is a man of a tribe and a clan and a house (even of "a door") as they are. Nothing could make him more human than that. Would the Masai people whom I have evangelized believe that Jesus is God? I would say, yes, but that is not the way they initially think of him today, nor was it the way they first thought of him when first they heard of him. It took a long time for them, in community, to take that giant step to his divinity. Perhaps no longer, though, than it took the original disciples and followers of Jesus to come to it. How long was it for them? Wasn't it at least thirty years after Jesus no longer walked among them and talked with them, that they first began to write down the meaning of that life that had been lived among them? Didn't it take thirty years of reflection on the life of the man Jesus, before they could come to the realization and conviction and courage and faith to say, "It is the Lord"? "It is the Lord who was among us."

There was no other way for the disciples of Jesus to come to know him, except through the human life he lived among them. No other way to come to the deepest meaning of what lay within, except by reflection on what was clearly visible and audible and sensible and touchable without.

And there is no other way for the Masai of today to come to

the fullest meaning of what happened back there in Galilee long ago. It is a tragedy that those young people in that classroom in America never had the opportunity to come to know Jesus in the same way. If they had, perhaps they would have had a different answer to the question: "What do you think of the Christ?"

Jesus is recorded as asking that question of his own disciples in his lifetime, and the answers he got were not exactly reassuring. Only one in the crowd came close. That one at least placed him as the Jewish Messiah, which is not the same thing as the Lord. That difficulty is recorded as continuing into the resurrection stories, the terrible difficulty of recognizing the Lord.

Of course, Jesus didn't help matters by the way he asked the question that day. He did not refer to himself as the Lord, or even as the Christ. He called himself, as he always did, the son of man, the son of Adam, the human. With that decidedly weighted description, it was a little difficult to answer the question, "Who do you say that I am?"

When I began to speak with the Masai people about Jesus, I kept that question always in my own mind, and I tried to plant it in the minds of the Masai, to be kept there for constant referral. "What do you think of this man Jesus I am talking about, this *oltung'ani Yesu*, this son of man, this human? Who do you say that he is?"

Perhaps it was in this area of trying to impart to the Masai people what I knew of Jesus of Nazareth, more than in any other work I have ever done, that I felt most in contact with the church that had sent me, with the generations and generations of people who had gone before me. The Catholic church used to talk about "apostolicity" being one of the "marks" of the true church of Jesus Christ, that is, an unbroken chain of hands coming down from the apostles even unto our age. I think "apostolic" is truly a mark of the authentic church of Jesus, but I believe it is rather a question of being apostolic in the sense of witnessing to the same Jesus the apostles witnessed to, or better, in the sense of evangelizing, preaching the gospel to the world that never heard it, as the apostles did. Being missionary, that is. That is the mark of the true church of Christ.

It was this area of talking about Jesus with the Masai that was the most exciting and challenging and revealing and richly rewarding. It would be far beyond the scope of what I am attempting in this writing to recount in detail all the steps necessary to expound the mystery of Christ to any people, Masai or otherwise. But I would like to touch on some of those aspects involved in the task which were unique and peculiar and necessary to the Masai.

The first thing I had to do was establish the reality of Jesus, both human and historical. To accomplish this for the Masai who were illiterate does not entail the same process as it would in doing so for people who have libraries and newspapers and television sets. I tried to go about it by speaking with the Masai in this way:

"The man Jesus was a man from a tribe who lives far away from here. Actually he was a member of the tribe of that patriarch Abraham that I had spoken about, the one who led the human race in search of the High God. We really don't know very much about the birth of Jesus or his childhood, or even about the time he was a warrior. (There is no word in the Masai language for 'teenager' or 'youth'. Every male teenager or youth is a *warrior—ol murrani.*) We do know, though, about his background. He came from a good family. It was his tribe's custom to keep a list of one's ancestors, even to write their names down in a book. So we know the names of his forebears. Some of them were very distinguished, like Abraham himself, one of the founders of the tribe. His tribe was called the Hebrew tribe, the Jews. A son of Abraham was named Israel, so the tribe is sometimes also called the tribe of Israel. There are twelve clans in the tribe of Israel."

Clans are very important in the Masai tribe. There are also twelve clans in the Masai tribe. One of the first questions a Masai will ask of a strange Masai is what clan he or she belongs to. A boy will especially ask a strange girl this question, because marriage is strictly taboo within a clan line.

"Jesus was of the clan of Judah. There were some very famous men in that clan—wise men, brave men, good men. One door (house, family) of that clan was so wise and brave and good that men of that door were chosen to be legwanan (chief) generation after generation. I know that among you Masai the rank of legwanan is not hereditary. It comes to a man of an age group who is gentle, above all, who can keep his head when others are losing theirs. It is bestowed on a man who is brave, wise, and eloquent. He is both proud and sad when he is chosen legwanan, proud to lead the brothers of his age group (orporor), but sad because he knows he will be the first to marry in his age group, first to own cattle, first in the line of battle, and first to die—all for the sake of his brothers. He leads them through life and even into death. In Jesus' tribe, the rank of legwanan was hereditary. That makes it no less beautiful, no less sad.

"It became hereditary as an honor bestowed on one of the greatest legwanans in the story of the tribe, a man called David. Even as a warrior he was a very brave man. As a young warrior he singlehandedly killed a lion which was attacking his flock, just as many of your warriors have done. A good shepherd does not run away when lions come. David also led his people into many battles in war and brought them out victorious even over their fiercest enemies. The young girls of his day used to sing songs praising him. (Almost the entire repertoire of songs of young Masai girls deals with the praising of warriors.) His name was known. David was the greatest legwanan the Jewish tribe ever had. They called him the 'lion of the clan of Judah.' Jesus was of the door and family of David.

"Jesus was circumcised to become a full-fledged member of the Jewish tribe. He lived long ago, before the first known age group of the Masai. He lived in the country of the Jews, in a town called Nazareth. People called him Jesus of Nazareth."

Circumcision was very important for the Masai. Since the Masai cannot count over one hundred, the expression "two thousand years ago" would be incomprehensible to them. They do have a way of keeping historical time, by means of the age groups, each one spanning seven years, and each one with a different name. By this method they can place historical events back to several hundred years ago, but not beyond.

Because of these details which I gave them, they now had a sense of the human-ness and reality of Jesus, as convincing to them as a photograph or a biography would be to us. What remained now was to try to explain to them the meaning of the man Jesus.

The Word Made Flesh

I spoke before about the necessity of peeling away from the gospel the accretions of the centuries, and of Western, white, European, American culture, to get to the kernel of the gospel underneath. This involves separating it from the philosophies and theologies with which we have long identified it—even from good philosophy and good theology.

We can be proud, in our Western culture, of the levels of philosophical understanding which we have brought to the message of the gospel: Trinity—one nature, three persons; transubstantiation—accidents of bread enduring through a change from substance of bread to that of the Body of Christ; hypostatic union—one person of Jesus Christ with two natures, human and divine. The very notion of *person*, so rich and meaningful in our culture today, comes from the philosophical and theological discussions of the church concerning the meaning of Father, Son, and Holy Spirit. Before those discussions began, there was no such notion in the Latin culture which gave us the word *persona*. *Persona* was a mask with which an actor covered his entire head, a different mask to portray each different part.

Persona in no way represented what we would call the real personality of the character portrayed, or of the man behind the mask.

But one great difficulty in identifying these concepts, as beautiful as they are, with the Christian gospel, is that it would necessitate one's being a teacher of scholastic or Thomistic philosophy even to begin to understand the message of Christianity. They are concepts entirely wedded to Western, Greek, and Roman culture.

The Masai life, like all human life, is riddled with disturbing, haunting questions. The Masai look around at all the kinds of things they see on the earth—the mountains and fields and streams and the wild animals, that great mass of wild game, and the cows and goats—and in the middle of it all, man, the Masai. What is man? As he lives and moves about on the earth, what is he? He does not live for very long really, a little longer than the animals, but not as long as the mountains and the trees. Why does he grow old so fast? Is there nothing before he is born and after he dies? Just a brief period of light between two periods of darkness, like a fire that sputters for a few moments and then dies out? Darkness before and darkness after? That fire really does not have much meaning, except for a few minutes. Does his life have any more meaning than the fire? It burns a little longer.

What does life mean? Here he is living on the earth. What should he do here? In all his life he is asking that question. Should he be like the animals, eating, drinking, sleeping, giving birth, and dying? Can't life have some meaning, at least for the short time he is here?

Sometimes life does have meaning. When he does a particular work well, it has some meaning. When he finishes building a beautiful, circular kraal; when, because of his effort, cows are healthy and there is milk; when he is healthy and he has many happy children, life does have meaning.

When a child is born; when there is a big happy feast day on which a name is given to a child newly born; when a young man or a young girl is initiated; when two people are married; at the *eunoto* ceremony, when a new young elder is blessed with milk; when all the mothers are blessed for fertility; when a woman is about to give birth, and the cycle of life begins again. Sometimes there is a lot of meaning in life.

Still, he lives in a kind of darkness with so many unanswered questions. Why in the midst of all these good things are there so many bad things? Look at all the trouble people cause one another. They argue and fight and hate and beat their wives. And others come from afar and fight with them and try to steal their cattle. And wild animals come and eat the grass the cattle should have, and some come and try to kill the cattle. Why does he have to build a big wall around his home to keep out wild animals and thieving humans? Why does the grass dry up? And the water? And the rains not come, leaving the people hungry? And those beautiful children who are born, and the mothers who bear them—why do they die so often? And the stately warriors, why do they so often fight and hurt each other and other people, and kill other people and be killed by them?

What kind of a world is this? Is it just a place where people are played with and teased and crushed with sorrow and given many glimpses of happiness only to have it taken away? And why the shadow of death hovering over all people? Is there really any meaning in life after all?

And God, Engai? What is he really like? Does he love all Masai, all people? Is he kind sometimes and cruel at other times? Does he always give everyone his just rights? Does he talk with people? Or can't he? Does God live far from here? Does he still work among the Masai, or has he forgotten them? Does he help just the healthy and the rich, or would he be willing to help a poor sick man without any cattle? Does he ever answer any of these questions? Or is he a mute God?

For the Masai some of these questions are spoken out exactly in this form. Other questions are asked in a more indirect way.

But all of them are there. It is to these questions that I spoke when I began to tell them of Jesus.

"This is the news I bring. The word has gone out over all the earth, and I believe it, that in the man called Jesus, from the town of Nazareth in the country of Jews, God has told us what he is like, has shown us who and what he is. The word is that Jesus is the answer to your questions and mine. For a few short years, which seem like only a few seconds in the life of any man or any people, Jesus pulled aside the dark, heavy clouds that hide God from us, and for one, brief, shining moment showed us a glimpse of God, showed us what God is, what he is like, how he feels.

"The God that Jesus tells us of and shows us is so different from the God we had imagined with our own minds that it takes your breath away. If what Jesus says about God and shows us about God is true, then we can only say we would never have known about this God without Jesus, that this knowledge of God was like a secret hidden from the beginning of the world until now.

"What does Jesus tell us and show us about God? First he tells us that God is not one who lives far from us, one who sees all the evil in the world and just passes by. Jesus tells us that evil is not from God. He does not make evil. He hates evil. He fights against evil. He wants to destroy evil and wipe it out, not just for one or two people, but for all the people of the world, not just for one day or one year, but for always.

"Jesus shows us that God is affected by the suffering of one human being. He is so touched with mercy at the sight of human beings' suffering that he wants to wipe out this suffering, not by sitting far off and working an occasional miracle, but by coming among us, sharing our life with us, suffering with us every sorrow we have ever known, so that he might wipe out suffering completely. That is why he created in the beginning. That is why he is creating now. That is why he continues to create until his

work of creation is finished, and he will save the world. That is
what it means to create the world—to save it.

"Jesus learned more about God every day of his life, and he
continued learning until the end. And so must we. He showed us
that no one can completely understand how deep God is, how
wide he is, how wise he is, or the knowledge and the plans he has
for the world and for us. No human mind can completely
understand the mind of the High God, so great is it. Not even
the son of man, the mind of the man Jesus, can know the day or
the hour that God will bring the world to completion, finish the
work of creation is finished, and he will save the world. That is
God. But what we can learn of him is enough to fill our minds
with peace and joy and happiness like we have never known.

"God has no arms, no hands, no legs, no body. He is like
breath, like the wind—invisible. How can he become visible in
the midst of all the things he created? How can he know what
suffering is? How can he feel merciful towards our suffering?
How can he share it?

"If God wants to be visible, to appear in the midst of creation,
there is only one thing he can do. He must take on human flesh.
He would have to create human flesh in his own image and
likeness. And he did. He made man in his own image and likeness, to walk the earth, to subdue the earth and save it. This is
what Jesus has shown us, not only about God, but about man.
Not only is God different than we thought. So is man.

"Man is not just like a fire sputtering for a few moments, then
fizzling out, darkness before and after. Man is not the plaything
of the universe, not a thing to be teased with happiness and
crushed with sorrow, a thing without meaning among the many
things of the earth. *Man is God appearing in the universe,* appearing visibly in the midst of all he created. That changes the meaning of man, doesn't it?

"I can see you Masai shaking your heads and saying, No! Man
is not God. We know man, and he is filled with evil. He fights, he

kills, he destroys, he does everything to separate others, and to separate himself from them.

"I say to you Masai: you have not known man, you have never seen a man. Creation is not yet finished. What you see is creation groaning and moaning even until now, yearning to be finished and completed, to be the body of God.

"But suppose the fullness of time had come and the work of God was perfect, and there appeared a man who was perfectly a man, according to the plan of God, a man completely human. If, once upon a time, there was such a man who was so completely a man, so perfectly human, then there would be no other way to describe him than to say: this man is God—God appearing in the universe. Isn't that so? Jesus was that man.

"Perhaps the really surprising thing that the man Jesus did in his lifetime was to show us, not only what God is, but what man is."

He Spoke to Them in Parables

The Masai are, by and large, an illiterate people. The method of preaching the gospel to a people in that situation is necessarily different than it would be to people with literacy—books, magazines, and libraries. The importance of the written gospels necessarily diminishes in such a condition. Underlying these four gospels is a message for mankind. It is this underlying message that the missionary has a responsibility of imparting to people who have never heard it. He has no such obligation towards the four gospels. The first generation of Christians lived without these written gospels, basing their lives on the basic message of the gospel. It was out of these communities, born in response to the simple gospel message, staking their lives on this message, and forming their lifestyle according to it, that the first written gospels emerged.

Any one of the four gospels represents a step into a cultural interpretation of the original gospel message. St. John's gospel is a masterpiece of adaptation of the Christian message to the Greek culture in the terms of Greek philosophy. It also carries with it not a little trace of anti-Semitism, another cultural interpretation. Each one of the evangelists had a specific purpose in writing down his gospel, a particular viewpoint to expound. The supposition that the entire bible existing at that time (Old Testament) was written solely for the purpose of supplying examples with which to explain the New Testament is a result of one such viewpoint. The important treatment given to Pontius Pilate (Roman and pagan) by the evangelists is an example of their awareness of the sensitivities of the pagan Roman peoples they were evangelizing. One does not have to give a course in Jewish history and geography and sociology before commencing the process of evangelization.

Of course, Jesus is at the heart of the gospel message. In the churches of Africa in the early centuries of Christianity, as well as in other churches of the known world, books and libraries were not so plentiful as they are today. Some church communities were not fortunate enough to own a bible. And that valuable possession was often stolen from other churches who once had it. When some of those early, bible-less churches used to gather for liturgy, the leaders often asked those assembled to recite or recall all the important stories and events in the life of Jesus. When they all had contributed what they knew and remembered, they had the equivalent of a gospel for that liturgy. It served the purpose that our scripture readings and liturgy of the word do in our liturgies.

For the illiterate Masai, no other method could better serve our purpose. I would try to convey to them what I knew from the written gospels and simply ask them to recount afterwards what they remembered of the stories and sayings of Jesus. Even as pagans they sat around at our regular get-togethers, recounting and discussing the stories of Jesus as they heard them. In the future, if they came to believe in Jesus, they would be able to gather as Christians and do the same thing, each one contributing what he or she knew and remembered about Jesus, and when, as a community, they had finished this, they would have their gospel, their scripture reading, their own liturgy of the word.

Illiterate people have remarkable memories. The more educated they become, the more their power of memory fades. The time of the fading of the memory would be an excellent time for the introduction of the written gospels. Perhaps the early Christians felt the same way. As the walking storehouses of personal experience with the man Jesus, those witnesses to his life, began to die off, the survivors began to feel the need to write things down. It presents an evangelist with an increasing challenge. What would you do if you had the task of presenting, just one time, to a people who never heard of it before, the message of Christianity, the story of Jesus. What would you pass on?

What I had to pass on, I had to present to the people sitting in front of me, the Masai of East Africa. I had to plant the seed in the Masai culture, and let it grow wild.

For many reasons I did not think that the birth, childhood and youth of Jesus had much to do with the message, so I started the story of Jesus when he was an elder, when he began in public to preach the gospel of the kingdom.

I told the Masai that the man Jesus, from the first day of his elderhood until the last day of his life, spoke of the land of green pastures that God is preparing for all the peoples of the earth, a land of incredible richness, a land and a state of peace and love and justice and truth. God himself is the shepherd of that land.

This is what Jesus told us about God: He said God is one who loves the poor with a special love. He is preparing the rich land for them. He loves the meek, the humble, the little ones. He will give them the earth. God loves those who mourn, those who are crying now. He will dry their eyes. God loves those who hunger and thirst after justice without getting it, those who suffer unjustly. He will satisfy them. God loves the merciful, who do not try to get their own back, do not seek revenge. He will be merciful to them. God loves those who are persecuted on this earth. He is preparing the rich land for them.

I asked the Masai if that is what they thought of God before they heard the words of Jesus. Does God love the rich, the ones with many cattle, the great and powerful? Does he love those who have much reason to laugh, those who get their due on this earth, who get everything coming to them? Or, does he love the poor, the little ones of the earth, the ones without any power, those who have reason only to cry, those who never seem to get a fair share of anything? With our poor heads, we might have answered one way. With the word that Jesus brings us, we have to answer another way. Who are the lucky ones, who are the blessed ones?

"Blessed are the poor in spirit. Blessed are the meek. Blessed are those who mourn. Blessed are those who hunger and thirst after justice. Blessed are the merciful. Blessed are those who are persecuted. God's rich land of green pastures is theirs."

Of course, there is no future tense in the Masai language. To convey a sense of future you have to use adverbs or some other word construction—"always, tomorrow, one week, one year, one day." "God loves the merciful. One day he is merciful to them. God loves the poor. He is preparing the rich land for them." I think you could say that one of the purposes and goals of evangelizing the Masai is to put a future tense in their language.

There is no sea anywhere near Masailand, no word in their language for it, no experience of fish. "The people of the green pastures of God are like a huge herd of animals," Jesus said, "which God, to keep safe from the lions, encloses in a large kraal, all together—sheep and goats, good cattle and bad cattle.

"The rich, green pasture lands of God are like a diamond or a ruby (well known in Tanzania). A man would sell all his cattle to own such a stone of great price.

"The green pastures of God are like a wedding feast or a

circumcision feast, where there will be dancing and singing, and sugar cane for the children to suck on, and beads for the women, and tobacco for the elders to chew on, and milk and meat for everyone. And honey beer. And many will come from beyond the white mountain of Kilimanjaro on the one side, and from beyond the Serengeti plains on the other, to rejoice at that feast."

There were three stories I used to love to tell the people. I have heard them retelling the stories, playing them back, so to speak. They grew richer in the retelling, for them and for me.

One was the story of the old man and the spittle, the story of God being like an old man with two sons, one a good brave warrior, and the other a lazy herder, who ran away in disgrace. It was the story of the father going up on the hill each night to ask for the spittle of forgiveness for his wayward son, and of the son finally returning to the village and the father running to meet him, to spit on him. Finally it was the story of the father's explanation that the spittle of forgiveness had been given him, and that his son who had been an outcast, a lost sheep, a dead person, had come back to life.

Another was the story of the witch doctor and the tax collector going to pray at the Masai equivalent of a temple, the volcano, Oldonyo L'Engai.

And then, the most popular story of all, the story of the Good Olmeg: One day Jesus told the people, "We must love God and love our neighbor as we love ourselves." Someone asked him, "Who is my neighbor?" and Jesus told this story: "Once there was a man making a safari from Ngorongoro Crater (a famous animal reserve and tourist attraction) to the place of Loliondo. On the way, he was attacked by thieves, robbed, beaten, and left for dead, food for the hyenas. A laibon passed by in his fine witch doctor robes, and when he saw the man, he passed by on the other side. In the same way, a legwanan came to the place, but when the chief saw the man lying there he also passed by on the other side. Finally, an olmeg (farmer, barbarian, 'dark, evil one') came driving by in his Landrover, and when he saw him he was moved with pity. He stopped and went to him, cleaned his wounds and gave him medicine. He put him in his car and carried him to the hospital in Loliondo. He said to the doctor there, 'Take care of him, and when I return, I will pay his bill.' Now do you know who your neighbor is?"

Africans love anything in the form of a riddle. They derive the keenest intellectual enjoyment out of a story told to them whose meaning is left for them to unravel. Perhaps the most effective way of getting across the force of Christ's parables is to tell them vividly and meaningfully, and then to stop dead, with little or no explanation of the meaning of the parable. "He who has ears to hear, let him hear."

*   *   *   *

Having explained not only what Jesus said, but, even more importantly, what he is and had done to him I finished the story of Christ for the Masai. They first laughed in disbelief at the crucifixion, as pagans will; then came to be scandalized by it, as religious people must. They will never take it for granted. And this people without a future tense in their language will be wondering about the resurrection the rest of their lives, as all believers should. This was the end of the good news I had come to proclaim to the Masai. The response to it was up to them.

6

The Response

Church

I mentioned that after having explained God and Jesus Christ to the people, I had come to the end of the good news. It might seem a bit abrupt, but I believe it is true. After proclaiming all that God has done in the world because of his love for the world and for human beings, and after announcing the depths to which this love has gone in the person and love of Jesus Christ, the missionary's job is complete. What else is there?

The church? Church-planting and church-establishing have often been used as descriptions of a missionary's task. But such descriptions can be misleading since they necessarily imply a kind of fixed and predetermined outcome to the preaching of the gospel. Because a missionary comes from another already existing church, *that* is the image of church he will have in mind, and if his job is to establish a church, *that* is the church he will establish. I think, rather, the missionary's job is to preach, not the church, but Christ. If he preaches Christ and the message of Christianity, the church may well result, may well appear, but it might not be the church he had in mind.

If the missionary truly presents God and Jesus Christ, his work is certainly finished. The rest is up to the people hearing the message. They can either reject the message entirely, or they can accept it. If they accept it, what they must do is outlined in general in scripture, but that outline should not be considered part of the good news. I think it is rather the response to the good news. It is the church.

While the general outline of the church is certainly present in scripture, the specific details of the church, the response to the good news, will just as certainly have to be as free and diverse as all the separate cultures of the human race.

What does scripture say people must do if they accept as true God's revelation to man? First, they must believe in all that God has done, and in Christ. Then they must be sorry that they have thrown this goodness back in God's face in ingratitude; they must be sorry for the part they have played in destroying the world and their fellow men. They must believe the unexpected good news that though they have taken part in this destruction, there is no reason to despair, there is no reason for anyone, or any people, to remain a failure forever. Because of Jesus Christ, all this can be undone, can be forgiven, and they can begin again anew. They must signify this belief and sorrow of theirs outwardly through a sign that all can see, that is, they must be baptized. They must not keep all this to themselves. They must go forth in the Spirit and witness to this good news and to Jesus, letting others see the meaning of it all, by their words and by their lives, until the time that Jesus comes again. And this is the final obligation: they must believe that Jesus will come again in consummation, and they must work in expectation of that parousia.

And that is it. That is the church.

Christ himself explained it very briefly in the first public words attributed to him: "The kingdom of heaven is at hand. Repent and believe in the good news."

The Acts of the Apostles expands this only a little in the teaching of Peter and Paul: If it is true that God has done all this, we must believe and repent of our sins, knowing that forgiveness is now possible through faith in Christ. We must go forth in the Spirit to witness to the name of Christ before the nations, until Christ comes again.

Repent, believe, be baptized, witness to Christ in the Spirit until he comes again. This is the response to the Christian message. That is the church.

Such a description of the church is both rich and deep, and yet free and open. It by no means leads one to come automatically to the form of the Western, Roman church we know, nor to the parish church we live and work in.

Historically, a single form of this response to the Christian message has grown and thrived. It is a response embedded in the culture from which it arose, with all the social, moral, and power structures of that culture remaining intact. It is the white, European response, with its Roman-Byzantine face. Until now that is the only response that has been allowed to the Christian message. That is the church we know.

What we are coming to see, now, especially in this context of bringing the Christian message to pagans of many different cultures, is that there must be many responses possible to the Christian message, responses which are filled with promise and meaning, but which have hitherto been neither encouraged nor allowed. We have come to believe that any valid, positive response to the Christian message could and should be recognized and accepted as church. That is the church that might have been, and might yet be.

We bring the Christian message to a pagan people. They accept that message. Their acceptance, their response, whatever it might be, is the church. They may be a people without prominently visible structures. Or they may be a pagan community with structures and lines of authority clearly drawn. Structured or not, they have a vision of the world and a style of life of their own. They hear the Christian message and accept it. They especially accept Christ with all that he means to that world vision of theirs in all its dimensions, and to their lifestyle. As they now stand, they are the church.

Institutionalized and structured in a way entirely different from ours, or noninstitutionalized, nonstructured and nonorganized, this response of theirs, as strange as it might seem to us, must be recognized as the church, or we are doing violence to

Christianity. Tillich says that beyond everything else, the church is simply and primarily a group of people who express a new reality by which they have been grasped.[1]

The earliest descriptions of the church paint a picture of community that is simple but filled with all kinds of possibilities for the nations and cultures of the world. "And the churches grew and expanded in numbers daily; and they continued in the teaching of the apostles, in the life of the brotherhood, in the breaking of the bread, and in the following of the Way" (Acts 2:4-2).

Community

It is a little difficult in America, in instructing individual "converts," or even groups of individuals in catechumen classes, to move towards the idea of a church that is a living community. Individual converts or groups of individuals are brought into an already existing organization, like people becoming members of the Elks.

It was not by any design on our part when we began the work of direct evangelization, but perhaps out of sheer necessity because of the structures of life in Africa, that we approached the people on the level of community, that is, on the level of a homogeneous group of people that considers itself a living, social organism distinct from other social groups. I see now there would have been no other way to work, no other way would have worked. I am quite certain no individual adult Masai would have agreed to participate in a lengthy, ordered dialogue and discussion between the Masai culture and the Christian message. He agreed to take this step only within the framework of his community, with his community, bringing his relations and relationships along with him. This was extremely important to my work.

I am saying two things: I could not evangelize the Masai in general, by bringing them into the mission, all coming from different sections of the five thousand square miles of the area. This would have been impossible physically, and it would have been the end of any dream of continuity or future growth. A mob has neither continuity nor homogeneity. And I could not evangelize them one by one, individually. There were thirty thousand of them.

But I could evangelize them in a community or in a series of communities. This is perhaps the most significant difference between what I used to try to do and what is being done today. What was impossible with an individual becomes amazingly possible with a community.[2]

Just what constitutes this workable community, it is difficult to say. It is not the tribe. That is too big. It is not even the clan. To recognize a community you have to ask yourself and others a few questions: If a man is part of a vital action taking place, either performing that action himself, or having it done to him, whom does this action affect in the same vital way it affects him? If a man were to kill or be killed, on whom does the effect of this action fall? Or, if a man were approached to become a Christian, who would be affected by his conversion, his baptism, his living out of his Christian convictions? His tribe? Hardly. His clan? No again. But there are people who would be vitally affected by an action of his, like conversion. And you could actually put your hand on those people if you get to know them even a little. That is his real community, certainly and infallibly. To find out what this community is, is necessary to this kind of work. Without finding it, and working within it, there is no possibility of evangelizing the Masai.

I am reminded of a very depressing experience I had while in America. I was working with a group of high school boys and girls. Together we were searching out the meaning of community in the midst of the tortured, fractured, temporary communities that make up the life of America. I picked out a girl at random and asked her, if something important should happen to her, who would be vitally affected by her action?

She said, "You mean if I committed suicide or something?" I agreed that would be a valid if somewhat morbid example. Without thinking another minute, she pointed to a friend, and said, "Mary here, and my mother."

That was all. No other person in that crowded room, no one else even volunteering to say he or she would be certainly affected. The others, in fact, agreed with her. If that was the limit of her real community, I could not even begin to imagine her life. Neither could I be sure that Christianity would be at all possible for her—or for the others. If she were at all typical of any segment of America, then I should think before anything else, America's greatest need would be first of all to find a sense of community again, or for baptized people, to find community again through Christianity.

Finding a real community among the Masai, I was able to teach them as a unit, to dialogue with them as a group, because there was a similarity of feeling and reaction among them. I noticed that every separate and homogeneous group among the Masai had its own character, its own reactions, quite different from other groups. I began to think of each group as a kind of distinct personality, much as I had been accustomed to doing with individuals in America.

One other thing I discovered. A community, a group like this, will act as a unit, accepting you or rejecting you together. I found out that change, deep meaningful change, like the acceptance of a hopeful, expectant world vision, does not take place in one individual at a time. Groups adopt changes as groups, or they do not adopt them at all.[3]

In approaching a legwanan (chief) and the ruling elders in the initial step and contact with a community, you are not really approaching individuals at all, but you are approaching the symbol of unity of a community, enabling it to respond as a unit. If you approach another individual, besides the leading elders, on your initial step, you might succeed in the end in "converting" that individual, but you have not approached the symbol of unity of that group. You have not, in effect, approached that community at all, and you have probably succeeded in effectively cutting yourself off from the possibility of ever reaching that group. You can expect them to resent and fight everything you do.

Seeing the difference between missionary work and pastoral work is important, and one has to analyze carefully the methods involved in both types of work to see if exchange is possible or desirable. While Holy Name Societies, women's guilds and youth movements might be beneficial to parish work on the home front, such divisions of a community might be inimical to the sense of community already present in an African group.

In my case, in Masailand, it would have been neither possible nor wise to try to evangelize the youth (warriors, in this case) directly. All the more unwise to deal directly with children—if I really wanted to reach the community. What I would be doing in appealing directly to youth (warriors) and children (as was previously done with the school system), if I would actually succeed in bringing them to Christianity, would be to make them outcasts of the community, outside the structure of the community. Until the community is Christian, they will be outcasts. And it is such individuals fighting against the structure of the community and the tribe who will most certainly follow the line of least resistance, and slide back to where they were, taking not much more with them than their Christian names and Western clothes. And so often you can chalk off the years dedicated to working with them as futile years, at best.[4]

I remember the young priest in America who told me of the two years he spent working with a black youth group. He spent all his energy, time and money in developing a basketball team. It was hard work, but at the end of two years he had a championship team. The night of the winning game, as they were all gathered in the rectory celebrating the victory, a call came to the rectory to the captain of the team. The message was: you and the others, drop that priest right now and come home "to the brothers," for good. They did. It was the last he ever saw of them.

We had always looked at the Masai and said, "It is the terrible indifference of the tribe that makes it so hard for an individual in it to be a Christian, the terrible inertia of the tribe." What chance does an individual stand in such a set-up? Precisely. That same inertia can turn into a dynamic vital force enabling an individual to cast off his despairing, hopeless, futureless vision of the world, and share in community hope. I know many individuals who would never have been able to take that tremendous step on their own. In community, they have.

In short, it is not possible or desirable to convert the Masai as individuals, but it is possible to evangelize them as groups. That might sound like a cliché, but I am convinced that individual conversion has been our policy up until the present time, and our mentality. Even now I do not think we are prepared to make the provisions necessary even to consider group evangelization of the Masai or any tribe. Our whole machinery is geared to individual conversions, our whole policy, our whole set-up and structure. The central mission compound is based on the theory of individual conversions, our catechetical and liturgical structure: individuals coming to the mission. An individual might walk twenty miles for instructions, but a community never would. A community does not travel to other places to worship. It worships where it is and as it is. Our seminaries and training of priests and ministers are based on the theory of individual conversions, individual vocations unrelated to community. If a large enough group accepted Christianity and baptism, it would be only natural to train a person in the midst of that community, for service in that community, not at some distant seminary. The reason he is sent to a seminary distant from the place where he lives, is because in reality he is not from that community situated where he lives, or from any community, as far as being chosen by a community or suited to a community, is concerned. His vocation is his own, individual affair. He is not trained for any particular community or group. He is trained on an individual basis, and then wished or imposed on some community that does not even know him, that may or may not like him, that may or may not find him suited to their service. Community service is the furthest thing from the minds of the planners of mission seminaries. Individual conversion of the seminarian, sometimes unrelated to Christian family or Christian community which might still be pagan, is often the basis of seminary recruitment. Individual holiness unrelated to community is the texture and fabric of seminary life. We would never be able to cope with community conversions or group conversions if they came. We would not be ready if they should happen.

The individualism which comes from our culture not only shapes the missionary who arrives on the foreign scene; it is part of the exported Christianity, in theory and in structure, he tries, with such good will, to pass on to a communitarian people.

A missionary facing an alien pagan culture, to be an efficient instrument of the gospel, has to have the courage to cast off the idols of the tribe, of the tribe he came from. There are many idols, but two which, I believe, particularly mesmerize the Western church, are individualism on the one hand, and love of organization on the other.

We consistently tend to interpret Christianity either from the individual or organizational viewpoint. The love of organization and power structures have led to our ideas of lord bishops and pontiff popes and national associations of the right and of the left and (especially since Vatican II) a plethora of meetings and chapters and synods and councils and committees. Individualism has its obsessions also: individual responsibility, individual morality, individual vocation to the priesthood, self-fulfillment, individual holiness and salvation. Individualism on one side, and organization on the other, with little room for community in between.

Besides paying lip service to the idea, how seriously do we consider the possibility that Christianity is essentially directed neither to the individual nor to the organization, but to the community?

Does Christianity make any sense outside of a community? Is baptism a call to individual salvation and self-fulfillment, or a joining of an organization? Or is it not an incorporation into a community, a community called to the salvation of the human race? Is the eucharist food for the individual soul, or the building up of an I-Thou relationship with Christ (or with anyone else), or the private domain of the priestly caste of an organization? Or is it not the sign and bond of unity and charity of a community? "This bread that we break, is it not the *koinonia* (brotherhood) of the Body of the Lord?" (1 Cor 10:16).

Can we really interpret the morality of sex or marriage, property, wealth, justice, neighborhood crime, punishment in prison, racism, war—from the point of view of individuals alone? Or worse, from that of organizations? Isn't that just what is so often wrong with our moral judgments?

Americans seem terrified of the anonymity of a community, and seek the value of personal fulfillment almost, as it were, against the community. Person is a Christian word, the very meaning of which is defined in relation to a community, beginning with the Trinitarian community outwards. There is no development of the person that is not directed towards the community.

Can the priesthood be interpreted from the point of view of an individual's sharing in the priesthood of Christ, through an individual call or vocation, a call that sets him above his fellow men in dignity and holiness? Isn't the Christian priesthood, in contradistinction to the pagan one, essentially a communal one, given to a community? Isn't the starting point community rather than individual? And it certainly has nothing to do with organization.

All Christians, as members of a community, are priests in the true sense of the word. The ministerial priest, by his ordination, does not become a better or holier man for it. He merely becomes essentially a community man, a servant of the community, a sign of the unity of that community, a focal point for that unity.

Very often we throw the word "priest" around in a seeming effort to justify anything we are doing, especially in the line of self-fulfillment. The scientific world, the political world or the educational world is very pagan and unchristian. So we say we need priest-scientists, priest-politicians and priest-teachers to minister to them. And herein we have our justification for all three. I think this is confusing the ministries of the church very badly. If these worlds are really pagan, they need a Christian who is an evangelist, not a priest. Evangelist and priest are two different functions in a Christian community. Except in the mind of those who would restrict all the power and the glory of Christianity to a single individual.

We Believe

As I was nearing the end of the evangelization of the first six Masai communities, I began looking towards baptism. So I went to the old man Ndangoya's community to prepare them for the final step.

I told them I had finished the imparting of the Christian message inasmuch as I could. I had taught them everything I knew about Christianity. Now it was up to them. They could reject it or accept it. I could do no more. If they did accept it, of course, it required public baptism. So I would go away for a week or so and give them the opportunity to make their judgment on the gospel of Jesus Christ. If they did accept it, then there would be baptism. However, baptism wasn't automatic. Over the course of the year it had taken me to instruct them, I had gotten to know them very well indeed.

So I stood in front of the assembled community and began: "This old man sitting here has missed too many of our instruction meetings. He was always out herding cattle. He will not be baptized with the rest. These two on this side will be baptized because they always attended, and understood very well what we talked about. So did this young mother. She will be baptized. But that man there has obviously not understood the instructions. And that lady there has scarcely believed the gospel message. They cannot be baptized. And this warrior has not shown enough effort . . . ."

The old man, Ndangoya, stopped me politely but firmly, "Padri, why are you trying to break us up and separate us? During this whole year that you have been teaching us, we have talked about these things when you were not here, at night around the fire. Yes, there have been lazy ones in this community. But they have been helped by those with much energy. There are stupid ones in the community, but they have been helped by those who are intelligent. Yes, there are ones with little faith in this village, but they have been helped by those with much faith. Would you turn out and drive off the lazy ones and the ones with little faith and the stupid ones? From the first day I have spoken for these people. And I speak for them now. Now, on this day one year later, I can declare for them and for all this community, that we have reached the step in our lives where we can say, 'We believe.' "

We believe. Communal faith. Until that day I had never heard of such a concept, certainly had never been taught it in a classroom. But I did remember the old ritual for baptism of children, the first question in that ceremony. "What do you ask of the church of God?" we inquired of the infant. Of course, he couldn't answer for himself. He couldn't speak for himself. He couldn't even think for himself. He certainly could not believe. And there is no such thing as a valid baptism without belief. Such an act would be magic, witchcraft.

The answer to that question, supplied by sponsors, was not "baptism" or "salvation." It was, "faith." That is what the child

asked of the church of God, of the community of believers—
faith, their faith, to become his, to make baptism possible.

I looked at the old man, Ndangoya. "Excuse me, old man," I
said. "Sometimes, my head is hard and I learn slowly. 'We believe,' you said. Of course you do. Everyone in the community
will be baptized."

It was in one of the five remaining communities in the final
step of preparation for baptism, that I came across a notion that
would be of extreme importance to the future evangelization of
the Masai.

I was speaking with a group about the response in faith that
they were about to make to the gospel, and I asked them, "If you
do accept baptism as a community, what will you call yourselves?"

There was, of course, no notion of church, or word for it, in
their pagan language. I had no idea of how to refer to them after
baptism. After some discussion among themselves, a man stood
up and said, "When we are baptized, we will become the *Orporor
L'Engai,* the age group brotherhood of God."

The age group brotherhood, the orporor, the most sacred
notion in their culture. It was a word that could grip their hearts,
set their hearts on fire, the single most important value in their
tribe. And they had chosen it as the word for *church.* Not only
was it the only notion of brotherhood they had, but it was one
that could not be acquired by birth, but only by deliberate, painful initiation. Their original notion of orporor was limited to all
those initiated within a seven year span, and those females who
married into the brotherhood. Every seven year time span had a
name which was never repeated. The orporor of God would not
span seven years, but would extend from now until the end. It
would, because of the message that brought it into being, cross
sex lines, age lines, clan lines, tribal lines, national lines. It would
be the first universal brotherhood, but it would necessarily still
be an age group brotherhood—of the last age, the final age of

the world, reaching to the kingdom. It has eschatological dimensions built right into it. There will be no danger that the Masai will ever confuse it in their thinking with a "church" building. It has come to be called alternately the orporor (age group brotherhood) of God, of Christ, or of the end.

In the evangelization of the Masai people, there has been no notion brought forward, with the exception, perhaps, of that of the "man Jesus," that has made them feel so certain that that which they have been treasuring and valuing for generations, has not been a waste, but rather a sign of God's continuing love for them, than the notion of the *Orporor L'Engai*. Perhaps for that reason, it lives today in Masailand.

Baptism

There was no need to explain to the Masai the symbolism of living, life-giving water. It was sacred to them long before I got there. Their word for God means rain—it being the most beautiful description of God they can think of.

The Masai being baptized would change their names, as they were accustomed to doing at any important changing point in their lives, like the Old Testament people—Abram to Abraham, Jacob to Israel. However, if they wanted to keep their old beloved names, I saw no harm in that. We needed some saints with names like Oltimbau and Kurmanjo in the litany of the saints. One thing they were not encouraged to do, nor did it ever occur to them to do, was to choose European and American names like most of their predecessors in other tribes of Africa, and school children in their own, had been subtly forced to do. They had some beautiful names in their own pagan language, and now they would be able to use them freely in the Orporor L'Engai— names which meant "God with us" and "gift of God," and "the beautiful one" for little girls, and "the brave one" for little boys.

The baptisms, as they took place in the six communities, were simple affairs, the bare essentials of the baptism ceremonies. I was afraid to take any steps beyond the bare essentials, for fear of cultural encroachment, even in the matter of such things as symbols to be used. Certain symbols might strike my fancy, and I might think they are very fitting. But it would be up to them, not me, to enhance those essentials in any way they wanted in later ceremonies, and enhance them they did, as the months progressed, into very elaborate baptismal liturgies. They were masters of liturgy in their own right, as pagans. Liturgy is part of a culture. So is a way of praying. Now that the gospel had come to them, they would have to have their own liturgy, their own way of praying. That was their affair. Mine was the gospel.

Even in some of those first baptisms they began to bring in their own signs, burning embers passed from one to another, all lighted from the same fire, itself lighted from two sticks of wood. Anointing with oil: sheep fat and other kinds, are liberally poured over Masai men and women at many important stages of their lives—warriorhood, motherhood, elderhood, when they are sick and in danger of dying. So it very naturally became part of the baptismal ceremony.

Their singing and dancing came into the baptismal ceremony. And their praying. An old man it was who prayed for all of us. Not every person, I was assured, had the power and facility to ask blessings from God. Only certain ones. This man was one of them.

In one of the baptisms a young elder stood up and tried to read from the bible I carried with me. I said "tried" to read, because I truthfully have to say I never heard a worse reading of the particular passage he picked out, which happened to be a passage from St. Paul. He hesitated. He made mistakes. He stammered. It's no wonder. He had never been to school. He had learned to read on his own so he could read at this service.

Another man spoke about the meaning of what we were doing, and the gospel as he saw it. He made no mistakes. He was eloquent. He has always been eloquent. That is why he is the speaker.

I suppose, of the six communities, the baptism that was most important to me, that meant the most to me, was the baptism involving the old man, Ndangoya, and his community. His was the first, as far as I knew, the first baptism of an adult Masai community in all of Masailand.

When the day of baptism came, I was amazed, as I am today long after, at how serious and sober and reflective those Masai were. We had gathered them near one of the permanent streams which flow into their beloved rivers of the Masai highlands, rivers which give life to their cattle, and then flow on down to Lake Natron and over to Lake Victoria.

When they were gathered on the banks of the stream, I spoke to them. It was really the first liturgical sermon I had ever given in the Masai language, because these were to be the first initiated into the Orporor L'Engai. I suppose I stammered and stuttered as much as that poor reader.

I said, "I have finished my last instruction in your village. I will never come back to teach anyone else here. From this day on, it is you people who must teach the word of Christianity. You must anoint the people with sheep fat. You must baptize them. The brotherhood is yours. I have seen that you understand and believe the gospel of Jesus Christ. Guard this gospel. Do not change it for anyone. It is all I have given to you. Even if a good spirit or a bad spirit were to come and preach a different gospel, do not listen to him.

"I will return to you another time to break bread together as Jesus told us to do. When one of you, or more than one of you, is ready to call this community together, and to lead it in the baptism and in the breaking of the bread, and in your life outside this meal of holy food, I will leave you and you will be on your own. Learn to stop depending on me today. Start depending on the one you receive today, the Holy Spirit of God.

"As of today, you have the power, as a community, to reach even to the seat of God, and to serve your fellow man, because you are a chosen tribe, a royal priesthood,[5] a nation that has been anointed, a people set apart. Once you were not a people at all. You were a people with a past and no future (nothing after today). Now you are the people of God. Now you are the Orporor L'Engai."

Some days there's just not much you can say.

All of the men and women of Ndangoya's community chose new Masai names, filled with meaning for their new lives. All of them except Ndangoya. He said to me, "Of all the stories you told us, one I like most. It attracts me, the story of the man who left everything and led his people from the worship of a tribal god in search of the unknown High God. If you permit me, I would like to be called Abraham."

And so, with the whole neighborhood and visiting neighborhoods watching, he stood in the middle of the stream, and I poured water from the stream over his head—"Ndangoya, son of Parmwat, chief of your people, Masai—I baptize you, Abraham, in the name of the Father, and of the Son, and of the Holy Spirit."

NOTES TO CHAPTER 6

1. Paul Tillich, *Theology of Culture* (Oxford University Press, 1964), pp. 40–41.

2. Donald A. McGavran, in *The Bridges of God*, develops this same notion and demonstrates that both sociologically and historically this is precisely the phenomenon which has taken place in the church from the beginning. The bonds of relationship between people vitally interrelated serve as the bridges to God. *The Bridges of God: A Study in the Strategy of Missions* (Friendship Press, 1955), 158 pp.

3. McGavran, *Bridges of God*, pp. 12–13.

4. Ibid., pp. 10–11.

5. The expression in Masai, "You are a royal priesthood—*kake irara iloibonak lo'laigwenak*," is a preposterous joining of two concepts which have never gone together in the Masai culture, that of witch doctor and chief. But because it is preposterous, it gets the point across most forcefully. The idea of a witch doctor, priest, is not bad in itself. What is bad is what it has come to mean in the hands of an exploitive individual. Now the whole community of believers has the priestly (witch doctorly) function, and the end result is princely. The two notions, strictly separated in Masai history, come together in fulfillment.

7

A Time for Laughter and a Time for Tears

The In-Turned Church

With the first Masai villages baptized, and many more now to be evangelized, I began to become familiar with the "choke law" of missionary work, according to which the pastoral work needed for new and many Christians begins to choke out the possibility of further evangelization. It was not only a problem. It became for me a personal temptation, to settle down with these beautiful, new, exciting Christians, instead of moving on, as I had to, to begin all over again somewhere else. Not to move on just because it was the overall plan I had worked out, but because I had a missionary responsibility to the whole area where I was sent, not just to one little section of it. I had seen this choke law at work in the parts of Africa where I had already been assigned, with the Christians taking up all the time of the missionaries, and the pagans of the same tribe, or even of other untouched tribes, being left to some vague future, to some indefinite plan of evangelization one hundred years from now.

Of course, I could not abandon the new Christians, because they had no priests to lead them in their new life. If they would have had priests I could have left them right then. It is too bad they didn't. As it was, I would have to take care of them in some way, even as the work of further evangelization had to continue. Somehow the two works had to be combined, since I could look forward to no increase in missionary personnel at that time. (This problem would force me back to reconsidering the very meaning of mission.) There would have to be a new concept, not only of pastoral work, but also of evangelization. Both would have to become as mobile and active as possible, one reacting on the other.

The word "mission" is used in different ways, so many different ways today, that it has almost lost its meaning. Its original meaning was "the act of being sent," and so we say the mission of Christ, the mission of the church. In times past, the plural use of the word—missions—referred to the foreign mission fields. In those foreign mission fields themselves, the word "mission" meant the plant or establishment (including the church building) where missionaries lived. In the ecclesiastically developed dioceses of Africa today, that use of the word has given way to the word "parishes." African bishops and priests do not like to think of their church establishments as "missions." I don't blame them. I don't think they are. I'm not sure they ever were.

The original meaning of mission is one of the most dynamic ideas imaginable. The second meaning of mission, that is, the church plant and establishment, is just the opposite.

To my way of thinking, in the long history of the African missions, one of the most static and paralyzing ideas in that history has been that of the mission compound. And it is strictly one of our own making. If you go through all the recorded details of the missionary activities of Paul's life, you find that he never built or established a mission. In his first missionary journey he preached only in synagogues scattered throughout the area. And he had no permanent residence.[1]

In his second missionary journey he is recorded as preaching by the river outside the gates of Phillipi, at private houses, at synagogues, in the market place, and in the areopagus.[2] On the third journey he preached in synagogues again and in a lecture room.[3]

Paul built no priest house or missionary residence in any place he went. He put up no buildings in which to instruct his catechumens. He built no church in which his new Christians could worship. In short, he neither built nor established a mission. *He* was the mission—he and his companions—a mobile mission, a temporary mission in any one place, a team in motion and movement towards the establishment, not of mission, but of an indigenous church, resulting as a response to his preaching of the gospel.

Paul's work resulted in the establishment of churches. We instead found missions.[4] A permanent mission necessarily carries with it the atmosphere of foreignness, of colonialism. The word "mission" should really mean something in action, in motion, in movement, as it did for St. Paul. Mission compound, on the other hand, implies that the movement has come to a standstill. In the latter case, it is no longer a centrifugal force reaching out forever, as far as it can. It becomes instead centripetal, attracting everything to itself. Instead of symbolizing movement towards another thing (in this case, church) it becomes itself the end of the line. African resentment at this missionary presence, in some places one hundred years after the initial foundations, is understandable to say the least. The word "missionary" is really a misnomer in this context. The command to go out and preach the gospel has become subtly transformed into "Stay here, take care of what you have. Let others come to you." Missionary movement comes to a dead stop.[5]

If the immobilization of the concept of mission is a problem in the foreign fields, it is more so on the home front. The appropriation of the word "mission" (probably due to the importance the word was given in Vatican II) to all of the work of the home front, and to much of the work done by so-called missionary congregations, results in a complete distortion of the word, an emptying it of all its meaning.

Mobile would hardly be the correct word to describe a great deal of that work. Mobility on the home front would imply, at the least, a movement outside the doors of the parish church to the surrounding neighborhoods, away from the limits of the diocese to the society in which it is situated. At the most in such cases mobility would imply a movement reaching to the ends of the earth. One cannot deny that the work in a parish or diocese in America *could* be mission, that is, a work involved in the missionary out-reach of the church. But if there are no signs there of mobility, of action, of movement to the world around it, one has to deny that it is mission.

Mission is the meaning of the church. The church can exist only insofar as it is in mission, insofar as it participates in the act of Christ, which is mission. The church becomes the mission, the living outreach of God to the world. The church exists only insofar as it carries Christ to the world. The church is only part of the mission, the mission of God sending his son to the world. Without this mission, there would be no church. The idea of church without mission is an absurdity.[6]

Despite the widespread and popular clamor to have every work considered as missionary, there is, at the same time, a real fear of mission prevalent on all sides, an unfaithfulness to mission. Where do you see this fear? Where is the evidence of unfaithfulness to mission? You see it in African priests and ministers unwilling to leave their mission compound of Christians, to go to a continent that is pagan, their continent. You see it in African bishops unwilling to send them. You see it in the distribution of priests and ministers in the world. You see it in the handful of missionaries assigned to the task of evangelizing four-fifths of the world that is pagan. You see it in the missionary congregations and societies of our day, which have suddenly discovered that their vocation is, after all, to the upkeep of institutions that have sprung up around them in the homeland.

You hear it in the arguments of theologians that we have no right to "impose" the gospel on the world, in their forgetting that four-fifths of the world has the right to hear that gospel, the right to be presented with the prospect of moving forward in a world with unlimited possibilities.

You see it in the American church which finds nothing wrong in spending ninety percent of its resources on itself. You see it in the scandal of missionary finance. You see it in the melancholy fact of the scarcely eighteen percent of the world that has heard of Christ, nearly two thousand years after the resurrection.

Sometimes I could see that fear in the very pagan communities I was evangelizing. As I moved away from the six African communities which were baptized, to begin the process of evangelization all over again with new communities, I noticed again in the new communities what I had seen in the old ones, that the distinct communities differed from one another in their communal characters and characteristics. Once again they reminded me of individual characters I had known in America. Some groups were zealous, others lazy, as a group; some were intelligent, others not so intelligent; some open and generous, others stingy; some adventurous and daring, others closed up on themselves and fearful. The gospel, coming to these differing communities, was responded to differently, depending on the communal character of the group hearing it.

I remember one group I encountered as I began to go farther afield. From the beginning they seemed narrow, suspicious, even grasping. They seemed to have an image of Christianity and its emissaries fixed firmly in mind even before I arrived on the scene, and nothing I did after I got there could change that image. It was very difficult going. They wanted immediately to throw themselves into an attitude of deep dependence on me, and nothing could shake them of this attitude.

They were certain that I was hiding something from them, misleading them with my words that I wanted nothing from them. They believed that I really came to get something from them—their land, or their children, and when I finally let them know what I wanted, they would decide whether to give it to me, and then could expect something in return.

They found difficulty with the concept of the mission of the church, with the idea that the community of believers, once baptized, took upon themselves the responsibility of reaching outward to those outside the brotherhood of the church. The idea of Jesus being a "man for others" might be a beautiful concept,

but it would not be for them if ever they should become Jesus'
followers. I spent a great deal of time with them, and when I
came to the response to the good news that would be necessary
on their part—belief, repentence, baptism, and witnessing to the
good news until Jesus came again—they balked, and I knew I
was in trouble.

How does one prevent a distorted meaning of Christianity
from creeping into a community right at the start? It is only in
the imparting of an outward-turned Christianity that we have
any hope of achieving Christianity. An inward turned Christianity is a dangerous counterfeit, an alluring masquerade. It is
no Christianity at all.

The salvation of one's own soul, or self-sanctification, or self-
perfection, or self-fulfillment may well be the goal of Buddhism
or Greek philosophy or modern psychology. But it is not the
goal of Christianity. For someone to embrace Christianity for the
purpose of self-fulfillment or self-salvation is, I think, to betray
or to misunderstand Christianity at its deepest level.

The temptation to look inward is one that affects not only
individuals, but also whole communities, parishes, dioceses. In
such cases the physical or spiritual well-being of the Christian
community becomes the very goal of the community, the whole
reason for its existence. Any ulterior motive for the community's
existence is completely forgotten. Indeed the only valid reason
for the community's existence is forgotten.

Christianity must be a force that moves outward, and a Christian community is basically in existence "for others". That is the
whole meaning of a Christian community. A Christian community which spends all its resources on a building campaign for its
own needs has long ago left Christianity high and dry on the
banks. Or all its resources on an education program or youth
program for that matter. A Christian community is in existence
"for others" not for "its own."

The universal church is not immune to the same weakness. It
is amazing, how, in every crisis in world history, the church has

the temptation to react in an inturned way. "Straighten out the calendar of the saints", it says, "or purge some of the more outlandish ones on the list. Reform Canon Law. Revise the seminary curriculum or structure. Make new laws about the priesthood or the religious life. Clean up the liturgy. Tidy up the sacraments. Be good and the world will come to you."

And each time the thing that causes the crisis is outside the church. Instead of reaching out and reacting to the crisis where it exists, in a realistic way, the church turns inward and cleans its own house. Some of that house-cleaning doesn't have very far-reaching effects, and the reforms never really touch the cause of the crisis. After a time, the revamped liturgy grows stale and boring; the eucharist ceases to be an *announcing* of the death of the Lord, the sacraments become magic again; ecumenism, forgetting its main purpose "that the whole world may believe" becomes clubby and suburban; and youth goes its own way. The ferment and change and revolution are outside, and an inward-turned church never seems to realize why its reforms do not touch the world.

Even now it is only our contact with the pagan world, with the world that is not Christian, that has kept us honest and true to ourselves. And it is when we have turned in on ourselves, and away from that world to which we were sent, that we have become stale and decaying and irrelevant. A church that turns in on itself is no longer a church. A church that turns in on itself will surely die. Many have died in history.

I had to face a judgment with this community in front of me that I never dreamed I would be facing. I had completed the instructions to the best of my ability. Now I had the dilemma of extending Christianity to those who conceived of it in the most selfish terms—or refusing it to them. I talked again with the leader of the community. Either I had failed to explain well enough what Christianity is, or they had failed to understand it. They seemed still to think of Christianity as a kind of material gain for themselves, and worse, only for themselves. When I mentioned again the obligation of spreading the gospel to those who have not heard it, the leader said he would be glad to do so himself, if I would pay him a salary for doing it.

I looked at him sadly, stood up wearily, thanked him for his time—and walked away.

Rejection

I had achieved a kind of confidence in my work, a level of skill in imparting the Christian message, even a maturity, I suppose, in being able to refuse baptism to some people, or at least to defer it. In the latter case I had time to prepare for the disappointment involved. I had seen it coming and had time to be ready. But an event occurred which took me completely by surprise.

I had got in the practice of finishing instructions in any one place, and then going away for a week or so to give the people time to make a judgment on the gospel, to accept or reject it. I had done this with one community which lived far from the mission compound. Reaching them every week meant a very difficult safari, but I felt it was worth it. The instruction I gave to the people of that community was my most carefully prepared work. I was anxious to see them again.

I found them all waiting in the place where I had been meeting with them every week. I greeted them and sat down.

"Well," I began, "you have heard everything I can tell you about the Christian faith. You have had a week since I last saw you to think it over together. Do you believe what I have told you? Do you accept Jesus Christ? Do you want to be baptized? Could you tell me your answer now?"

The legwanan answered slowly and clearly, "We have heard what you mean by the Christian message. For a year we have talked about it. We have looked forward to your coming each week. We have listened with great interest. We thank you for coming to us. We think we understand what you have said about Jesus Christ. But we cannot accept it. We cannot accept your Christ or believe in him. We do not want baptism. Forgive us—our answer is no!"

No! I couldn't believe it. I looked at the legwanan and then around at the others. They returned my look steadily and calmly. I looked down at the ground trying desperately to think of something to say. What had I done wrong? What was the weak point of my instruction? Or was it in me? Was I the wrong person to have tried evangelizing these difficult people? A whole year. How could they follow instructions for a whole year and then refuse baptism? It was one thing for me to refuse baptism to a group of people whom I did not consider ready for it. But it was quite another thing to have a group of people, whom I judged eminently ready for baptism, to refuse it on their part. A whole community refusing the Christian message after having heard it, refusing Christ. Somehow I had failed badly in the mission entrusted to me. I had personally never heard of this happening to any missionary before.

I realized that they were waiting for me to say something. I looked up at them again, even though they were now slightly out of focus. "Thank you, legwanan", I said, not knowing really what I wanted to say, "thank you, all of you. You have been a very attentive group and a very intelligent one. You have treated me with great respect and patience. I just realized that I have come here for no other reason than this—to tell you about the Christian faith. That is the only thing I came to bring you, as you know, not medicine or schools or tobacco or gifts. I have come a long way just for this. So if you don't accept this, I have nothing else for you, no other reason for bothering you. As a matter of fact, I have no reason for seeing you at all any more. I will go elsewhere to find if others want to hear the Christian message. And I do not think that any other Padri will come here after me.

Sometimes people have just one chance to hear the Christian message, and perhaps this was yours. Thank you for your patience and kindness and—goodbye."

I hurried away from the village and back to my tent. I was not conscious of the fact, nor did I remember until long after, that Paul himself had shaken the dust from his feet in defiance of the communities that had rejected the Christian message, and that Christ had advised his disciples to do much the same thing. I would not have had the heart to do any such thing, even if I had remembered. I just realized vaguely and dully that my work with these people was finished in a way that it was finished with no other people.

For untouched pagans there always remains that point in the future when they might hear the Christian message, and so they remain a potential field of work for the missionary. Again, if a missionary is running a school, his work with a people is never finished. He is looking to the christianization of those school children so that tomorrow he will have Christian parents. Then he must continue to look after those Christian parents and their children. There is no end to it.

But there was an end to my work with these people. There were no moves left to make. The only reason I came these thousands of miles was to bring them this Christian message. They rejected it. There was nothing else I could do. My missionary obligation to them was finished.

Perhaps the most important lesson I was ever to learn in my missionary life, I learned that day: that Christianity, by its very essence, is a message that can be accepted—or rejected; that somewhere close to the heart of Christianity lies that terrible and mysterious possibility of rejection; that no Christianity has any meaning or value, if there is not freedom to accept it or reject it. It is not an automatic thing, coming like a diploma after four or eight years of schooling and examinations, nor after one year of instruction. It must be presented in such a way that rejection of it remains a distinct possibility. The acceptance of it would be meaningless if rejection were not possible. It is a call, an invitation, a challenge even, that can always be refused. The Christianity of a born Catholic or of a produced Catholic (the result of an automatic baptism following a set period of instructions) which is never once left open to the freedom of rejection, to the understanding that it is a thing freely accepted or rejected—is a dead and useless thing.

Since that day, I have never seen those people of that village again, but I remember them as I remember no other people that I have come across in all my missionary years. For me, at least, they are distinct. They are unique. I feel a tremendous respect for them. They taught me something that no other people in Africa have ever taught me.

But it took a long time for that lesson to sink in. Day after day I found myself returning in thought to that moment at high noon in the hot equatorial sun when I heard *no!* for the first time. And I never remember any other time when the silence and the solitude of the African nights seemed so complete.

Ole Sikii

Paul, my Masai catechist, a young man with some education and catechetical training, was invaluable to me in my work. He understood the work, had a deep feeling for it, worked very hard with me, and possessed a sense of humor which helped tremendously during some difficult times. He enjoyed traveling and meeting different people and did not seem to mind the rigors of safari life. In every village we came to, he made friends with the people of the village, stayed with them and ate with them. I really saw no need even to wonder about his position, until one day in the midst of instructions a man asked him point blank, "How much do you get paid for doing this work?"

He, of course, received a salary as every African catechist did. It was not much by our standards, or even by African standards of employment. A certified teacher in a government school would get double or triple what he made. A cook in the town of Arusha would make more. But it was a salary, and I began to wonder about it from that moment.

What effect would the knowledge of his salary have on the people we were evangelizing? Would they think that was his motive for his belief in Christianity, for his willingness to spread it? He was the only Christian in his family. He had been to a mission school when he was a boy. Even though his home was five hundred miles away, the people soon found out about his whole life story around the fires at night.

If we were successful in our work of bringing about completely independent, indigenous church communities, what would happen to Paul if all of us missionaries were to leave? Who would pay his salary? I felt certain the Masai communities could not. And, after all, which community should? He belonged to no Christian community, having come from a pagan one. If you have ever been in mission territory you would know what a delicate problem this line of thought opens up. Missionaries rely heavily on paid workers like Paul.

I liked him very much and I did not know what course of action to take. During the first wave of evangelization I began to see some light on the problem. In Ndangoya's community, there was a young mother who was very intelligent. She was the first woman of all to speak out in public in our meetings with the Masai. At first, the elders seemed startled and even a bit upset at her brashness. Women were never asked their opinion about anything in public. It was not valued for much. But this bright young woman had no qualms from the beginning. She asked very penetrating questions. She made very clear-minded remarks. She understood the instructions as well as anyone in the community. It was not very long before the elders begrudgingly admitted this fact. In time, they even became proud of her.

She could not read or write. One day I gave her some drawings which more or less recalled the gospel matter that we had talked about. I asked her if she could help me with the children in the village. My instructions were geared to adults and sometimes I felt the children were being left out. Could she pass on the instructions to the children in such a way that they could understand them? She agreed, and from that time on until baptism and after, she began teaching the children the gospel. She treasured those drawings, and it was touching to drive up in the evening to Ndangoya's village, and find that Masai mother with a flock of children around her, with the pictures in her lap, keeping alive the apostolic teaching of the church.

By the time I started the second wave of evangelization among new villages, I had developed a different way of carrying on the dialogue with the Masai. I would look for someone in the very first meeting with a new people, someone who seemed to understand the message better than the others. At the end of the meeting, when the crowd had dispersed, I would ask that person to remain. I would go over what we had covered in the meeting, and ask him if, at the beginning of the next meeting, he could refresh everyone's memory as to what we had talked about. When he had finished doing this at the next meeting, I would take over and continue on with new things. In some places it was very difficult, if not impossible, to find such a person. In other places the system worked very well, and in such places, after many meetings, we had a pagan in the group who, unknown to himself, was a catechist in the making.

It worked in no place better than in the village where the woman Keti lived. Keti was also a young married woman, with two children of her own, one about four years old, and the other an infant perpetually strapped to her back. She also was extremely intelligent. Somehow she had learned to read, haltingly of course, the national language of Tanzania, Kiswahili. She even reached the point where she could read the scriptures in her own language—Masai. This was no easy feat. Some time later when she was a Christian, she was doing this in the midst of a liturgy at which some visiting Masai teachers and secondary school students were present. To say they were startled at her skill would be an understatement, since they could not do it themselves.

Keti began each meeting with her people by refreshing their memory on the matters we had talked about at the previous meetings. And then I would take over. As the months went by, her part in the meeting increased and mine decreased. Theoretically I concluded that when she reached the point at which she conducted the entire dialogue, the people would be ready for baptism. She taught not only in her own village, but began to teach in surrounding villages which were completely un-evangelized. Perhaps the most enduring image stamped into my memory, and the one which gave me the most personal satisfaction, was the picture of Keti, with her baby strapped to her back, climbing the hills to the neighboring villages to tell them the story of Jesus Christ. Among other things, it shattered the notion of the male-chauvinist Masai who would not even listen to a woman, whether or not she had something worthwhile to say. And more important for the future possibilities of a living church in Masailand, she was an evangelist, an unpaid evangelist.

Many more possibilities like this opened up as the months and years went by. None more important than the entrance upon the scene of Ole Sikii. One day, in the very first wave of evangelization in the Loliondo mission area, a visiting Masai elder attended the instructions taking place in the village of the old man, Ndangoya. The visiting elder listened very closely to the instructions, and when they were finished, he approached me.

"I think you should meet my son," he told me. I asked him why he thought so. He said that, having heard what I had been talking about with the people of that village, I would be interested in meeting his son, and he would be interested in meeting me. He said his son was a very religious person. His name was Ole Sikii.

He arranged for me to meet his son, and a few days later I

went to his village and was introduced to Ole Sikii. He was not a prepossessing looking person, not as handsome as the average Masai, and not as tall. He had an air of simplicity about him that was at once disarming and misleading. He remains to this day one of the most remarkable people I have ever met. Neither he nor his mother remembered exactly how many days he attended school, but it cannot have been more than two or three weeks at the most, in the first grade, or Standard One as it was called. At any rate he was not there long enough to learn to read.

He was not of the Laibon clan, but even as a young boy he showed an extraordinary interest in things religious. He had about him a strong and natural sense of religion, or piety, as the theologians used to call it. He was initiated as a warrior, and soon thereafter began to exercise an instinctive gift of religious leadership in his village. He began not only leading the village in prayers, but encouraging the people to pray, organizing them in prayer. Certain days in that village were set aside by him for thanksgiving, others for petition. Ole Sikii was a born liturgist, and he developed for the village people distinctive rituals—simple, symbolic, beautiful. After I got to know him, I was invited to some of these pagan liturgies, and I attended them. There was dancing and singing, ritualistic drinking, processions around the village, and many prayers led by Ole Sikii himself. It was remarkable the way the people followed his leadership without question, even his own parents. It was all a beautiful, if extraordinary, example of pagan religion at its best. Ole Sikii seemed to have a deep felt hunger for God, a craving I have rarely seen.

It was his father who first told me about the safari (pilgrimage) to Oldonyo L'Engai. At a later date Ole Sikii himself filled in the details. He was in his twenties when I first met him. Several years before, filled with all the stories and traditions of his tribe, he was consumed with the desire to see God, Engai, face to face. What better place to accomplish this desire than on the top of the active volcano, Oldonyo L'Engai? Oldonyo L'Engai is just one of the many features of an extraordinary landscape in Northern Tanzania which includes snow-peaked Mount Kilimanjaro, an extinct volcano itself, twenty thousand feet high; Ngorongoro Crater (or, more correctly, Ngorongoro Caldera, a volcanic mountain that caved in on itself instead of exploding outwards); the Serengeti plains, a vast level stretch of treeless grassland which, together with Ngorongoro, holds the largest concentration of wild game left in the world; and just behind Ngorongoro to the north, the ten thousand foot high Oldonyo L'Engai, "the mountain of God," a perfectly shaped, absolutely barren, conical volcano. The distinction it holds is that it is still active, exploding in fire and smoke and lava at regular, predictable intervals.

It is the most spectacular geological display in all of Masailand. It is no wonder that it was chosen by the Masai as the most ideal temple place for God on this earth. At certain catastrophic moments in Masai history, witch doctors were known to climb this mountain to offer sacrifice to appease the angry red God.

Ole Sikii shared the belief of the pagan Masai in a terribly remote God. He longed to see him. Would it be possible that Engai sometimes visited the earth and took up residence in his volcanic temple, perhaps at those times when the mountain exploded in fire and smoke? He decided on a dangerous course of action. He would go and see. Not when the fire was pouring out of the mouth of the mountain. No human being could live through that. But just before it exploded, or just after the fire died down, he would go and see if God was there. Oldonyo L'Engai was some seventy-five miles away from his village. It would require a safari of two days to get there and two days to get back. It was a lonely trek through a barren waste. All the grass immediately surrounding the mountain had been scalded away by the repeated outpourings of the lava. Even those people who lived close to the mountain moved away when an eruption was imminent. He crossed those empty plains alone, armed with spear and short sword and a little food. He would fast as part of his preparation to meet God. He climbed the lava ridged side of the mountain through the slag and the cinders to the very rim of the crater and looked down into the mouth of hell. (At least that is what it looks like from a small plane flying directly over the crater, as I have seen several times.) He waited through the days and through the fearful nights when no Masai would remain alone. He stayed awake for most of the three days, praying on the rim of the crater. He dozed off occasionally to get some rest during the daytime, so that he would be completely awake at night. He fully expected to see God.

I have often tried to imagine what thoughts must have gone through his mind as he awaited that terrifying moment when God would appear. He did not appear, however, and a disappointed, disillusioned Ole Sikii went down from the mountain and trudged his weary way homeward in a crisis of faith. What more could a human being do to deserve to see God?

More prayers in the village perhaps? More rituals and liturgies and feast days? More imploring of God, under the most beautiful title man could give him—Engai, rain—to come down like rain on the dry earth and the parched lives of his people, to water them and bring them back to life? A good, holy pagan was Ole Sikii.

He was in the midst of this feverish preparation of his people for the next visit of God to Oldonyo L'Engai when I first met him.

He was a very friendly person then, warm and almost always cheerful, as he is now. But there was a kind of sadness about him when I first got to know him. He had tried so hard. His conscience did not accuse him of any sin that would have kept God from him. His faith was shaken. Why did God hide his face from him?

I almost had to smile when I realized how strangely things worked out. One time when my faith was shaken, a pagan Masai elder passed on to me his deep and beautiful wisdom. Now I, a Christian evangelist, would pass it on to a pagan Masai warrior:

"Ole Sikii, you have tried as hard as a man can try. You left your father and family and home and went in search of God up that terrible mountain. You tracked and followed him to his lair, like a lion tracks a wildebeeste. But all this time he has been tracking you. You did not send for me or look me up. I was sent to you. You thought you were searching for Engai. All this time he has been searching for you. God is more beautiful and loving than even you imagined. He hungered for you, Ole Sikii. Try as we might, we cannot reach up by brute force and drag God down from the heavens. He is already here. He has found you. In truth, Old Sikii, we are not the lion looking for God. God is the lion looking for us. Believe me, the lion is God."

I told him of Jesus Christ and the message of Jesus that would mean hope to his people. I did not ask him if his people would like to hear the Christian message, or dare to suggest that I might instruct them in it. That would have been foolishness on my part, and blindness to the obvious gift and charism sitting before me in the person of Ole Sikii. I simply taught Ole Sikii himself, by himself. And he instructed his people in his own time and in his own way. I did not baptize them when they were ready. I baptized only Ole Sikii. He baptized his people in his own time and in his own way. The liturgy surrounding that baptism, enriched by the rituals to which that village was already accustomed, was their affair, not mine. Mine was the gospel.

What did St. Paul say to the Corinthians? "Were you baptized in the name of Paul? I am thankful that I never baptized any of you after Crispus and Gaius, so none of you can say he was baptized in my name. Then there was the family of Stephanas, of course, that I baptized too, but no one else as far as I can remember.

"For Christ did not send me to baptize, but to preach the good news" (1 Cor 1:17).

After his baptism, Ole Sikii accompanied me on many of my safaris. He was of immeasurable help. Later he went on safaris of his own to bring the gospel to distant villages. He was the first true evangelist among the Masai, sprung from a true Christian Masai community.

He learned to read on his own. He would spend hours at the mission of Loliondo, or near my tent, reading aloud from the New Testament in Kiswahili. He has become quite fluent and literate in the language, and in his own written language of Masai. He can translate, in writing, the scriptures from Kiswahili to Masai. He is a natural liturgist who has created many of the present day Masai Christian liturgies. He was the first minstrel to compose Christian Masai music for our Christian services.

He has now received further training in scripture, doctrine, liturgy and church history. He has since married. He was a pagan the year before I met him, a Christian a year after I met him, and he should have been a priest the following year. It is obvious that he is ready to be ordained a priest for his community. If it would not mean going into schism, we would ordain him tomorrow.

He is the kind of person who never ceases to surprise you. Not long after his baptism, there was trouble in his village. A leopard was making continuous raids on the village. A leopard can be particularly dangerous, maybe even more dangerous than a lion. It is quicker, more treacherous, and it seems to have a blood lust. A lion generally kills because it is hungry. A leopard does that and more. Sometimes it seems to kill for the sake of killing. In one Christian village that I knew, a leopard once came in at night, killed thirteen goats and ate one.

I was once present just after a group of young warriors tried to kill a marauding leopard with their spears, weapons which are usually very handy for lion killing. But this leopard was exceptionally crafty and swift. He would crouch in a cluster of bushes, then make a dash at the warriors. They tried to kill him with their spears, but he was too fast. He would leap out on them, maul a warrior or two, then quickly retreat to his bushes unharmed. The people in the village called off the young warriors and sent in a group of seasoned older warriors. Their leader told them to put down their spears, and take out their knife-like swords, razor sharp on both edges. When the leopard came out again, they rotated their arms like propellers and cut the leopard to pieces. When I arrived on the scene I discovered a group of mangled young warriors and a sliced up leopard. Masai warriors maintain a genuine respect for leopards.

It was a particularly mean leopard that was causing mayhem in Ole Sikii's village. Every night the animal visited, he got away with the spoils of his raid. Hunting trips were sent out in the daytime to no avail. They couldn't find him. He was well hidden. So one day Ole Sikii, not really thinking he would be very successful, went out with a little boy to see if he could find traces of the leopard in the distant woods where it was thought he would be hiding.

Since it was going to be a bit of a trek, he let the little boy carry the weapons, thinking to take them from him at the edge of the woods. But he got no farther than a small clearing quite close to the village. There, lying on the path at high noon was the killer leopard, with a chewed up goat being further torn apart by leopard claws and teeth. The villagers had made one mistake in their appraisal of the situation. It was not a male leopard at all, as they had supposed. It was a female, and her little baby leopard was lying next to her, enjoying lunch with its mother. Which made the situation much worse. The little Masai boy took off in terror, carrying both weapons with him. Ole Sikii was standing face to face, not with God whom he wanted to see, but with a ferocious mother leopard whom he did not want to see, at least not without any weapon at all on his person.

The leopard was upon him on the instant. The fist thing a leopard tries to do is to take out its enemy's eyes with its claws. So Ole Sikii had to cover his eyes with his hand to protect them, and he had to keep that one hand across his eyes most of the time. His other hand went for the leopard's throat. And so they wrestled on the ground in a contest of death—Ole Sikii and a writhing, biting clawing cat, one of the big three killers of Africa, which tourist hunters come so far to shoot. Ole Sikii won the contest. He choked and strangled the animal to death with his arm and hands. He took his hand away from his eyes for the moment of truth.

I was on safari in another place when it happened. When I returned, I heard the news and went immediately to the hospital to see him. He was bandaged and mangled and mauled with his face and arms and legs swollen from the poisonous scratches.

But he grinned when he saw me. A smile was never far from his face at any time, even at a time like this. I just shook my head in disbelief and said, "Ole Sikii! I don't think I would have come out on top if an ordinary tom cat suddenly challenged me to fight to the death. And here you go taking on a leopard."

He grinned again, and his disarming simplicity astounded me. A line of verse came back to me from my schooldays. I couldn't remember the source but it certainly fit:

"His strength was as the strength of ten, because his heart was pure."

It is the Mass

In the old Latin form of the Mass, the liturgy concluded with the words, "Ite, Missa est," which was mysteriously translated as, "Go, the Mass is ended." The meaning was clear enough, though: "For half an hour or so you have come apart from the world and your life to a holy place to perform a holy act, to fortify yourselves for your return to that life. Now the Mass is over. Go back to that life."

We missionaries, sometimes being very careful about the liberating message we were bringing to pagan peoples, were not so careful in giving them the Mass which should have been nothing but the celebration of that message. We tried to adapt it to them with symbols and gestures taken from African life, but it was more than a few symbols and gestures from that life that was needed. It was their whole life which should have been involved. For them, before we came among them, religion and life were the same thing. There was no vast separation between religion and life, as there was with us. Upon the acceptance of the Christian faith, they were a people ideally suited to the celebration of the Mass, of the eucharist. Their Mass could have been the simple celebration of their returning their whole life to God, symbolized and sacramentalized in the eucharistic bread and wine. Instead, it became something more formalistic, more rigid, more divorced from real life, than Roman rite ever was for us.

Believing truly that the way of praying and ritual were the people's affair, not mine—mine being the gospel—I was extremely cautious in passing on to the people the liturgy of the eucharist. It was a response to the good news they had heard, a celebration of their belief in the good news. By breaking bread together as a community, they would signify and effect the presence of the Risen Lord, as well as their own unity and love in the Brotherhood, in the Orporor of Jesus.

To take the first step in directing them how to do this ritually was filled with dangers. Any symbols or gestures I might choose, as proper liturgical celebration, could easily seem a cultural encroachment to them. Ritual, as part of a culture, was their affair, not mine. And even if they did accept the form of liturgical celebration that I picked out for them, they could just as easily interpret this as the essential gospel that I was passing on to them, and cling to it tenaciously and rigidly, as first generation Christians are prone to do, and pass on, from generation to generation, as gospel, something that is clearly superficial and nonessential.

So the first Masses in the new Masai communities were simplicity itself. I would take bread and wine,[7] without any preceding or following ritual, and say to the people: "This is the way it was passed on to me, and I pass it on to you that on the night before he died, Jesus took bread and wine into his hands, blessed them and said, 'This is my body. This is the cup of my blood of the New Covenant, poured out for the forgiveness of sins. Do this in my memory.'"

That served as Offertory, Preface and Canon. The people took it from there. It is extraordinary the way people will play the gospel back to you, if it is presented to them in an uninterpreted way. Some tremendous difficulties, some unanswerable questions, and some profitable insights came to light around the notion of the eucharist through this playing back of theirs.

Masai men had never eaten in the presence of Masai women. In their minds, the status and condition of women were such that the very presence of women at the time of eating was enough to pollute any food that was present. Hence, men could never eat with women. How then was eucharist possible? In their minds it was not. If ever there was a need for eucharist as a salvific sign of unity, it was here. I reminded them that besides the law of love which I had preached to them and they had accepted, I had never tried to interpret for them how they must work out this law in their homes and in their lives, and in their treatment of their daughters and wives and female neighbors (as sorely tempted as I had been to do just that). But here, in the eucharist, we were at the heart of the unchanging gospel that I was passing on to them. They were free to accept that gospel or reject it, but if they accepted it, they were accepting the truth that in the eucharist, which is to say "in Christ, there is neither slave nor free, neither Jew nor Greek, neither male nor female."

They did accept it, but it was surely a traumatic moment for them, as individuals and as a people, that first time when I blessed the cup, or gourd in this case, and passed it on to the woman sitting closest to me, told her to drink from it, and then pass it on to the man sitting next to her. I don't remember any other pastoral experience in which the "sign of unity" was so real for me. And I was not surprised some time later when a group of teenage girls told me privately that the "ilomon sidai" (good news), that I talked about so constantly, was really good news for them.

One of the effects of passing on an already interpreted gospel to a people is the effect such a process has on you. You can easily come to think that the interpretation you pass on is the only interpretation possible. I wonder how many of us just naturally think that baptism is simply the first, infant step in the Christian life, in church life, a tiny parcel patronizingly passed on to those who cannot understand any more than that, or are not entitled to any more than that; a kind of primitive first stage in the life of the church; a passive, receptive stage at that. But if you do not interpret the gospel as you pass it on, you are just as likely to experience an entirely different reaction to such a thing as baptism. These people considered baptism everything. If I was entrusting them with baptism, in their minds, I was entrusting them with the church, the total responsibility of the church.

They asked me, "What does it mean that we are baptized? Just that, that water was poured on our heads by you? Or does it not mean that we ourselves can now baptize? What does it mean that we are baptized? That we can receive eucharist from your hands any time you choose to come to visit us? Or does it not mean that we are a eucharistic people?" Implying, of course, that they should be able to confect the eucharist without me.

They were right, certainly. And I had to admit to them that they were right. It was not scripture or theology which prevented them from doing what they thought they had a right to do, but simply the history of a church imbedded in a single culture, with its own ideas, coming from that culture, as to what number of years of seminary training were needed to lead a community in the simple act of celebrating the Lord's Supper, as he told us to do. Any command of his to undergo academic training before attempting to break bread together is strikingly missing in scripture.

What these people were suggesting was that the church which sent me should have insured that its bishop (whom they found no difficulty in accepting as head of a larger Christian community) should have come to them to declare that they were, in fact, a fully-fledged, eucharistic, Christian community, just like every other community in the church. Surely that is essentially what ordination means.

Sometimes, in those days, my heart ached in its inability to love the church as it was, and longed to see and love it, as it was meant to be.

At one point I thought the people were badly confusing the meaning of the eucharist, or that of the church, or both. They already referred to the church as the *orporor,* the brotherhood. Now, from time to time, I heard them calling the eucharist the *orporor sinyati,* the holy *orporor,* or the holy brotherhood. They would ask questions like this: "Next time you come, are we holding or making the holy orporor?"

It did not seem to make sense until I remembered St. Paul's saying, "This bread that we break, is it not the *koinonia* of the body and blood of Christ?"

We used to translate that word *koinonia* in this phrase as *communion.* Hence, our expression "holy communion," and our lack of wonder at any deep mystery in the phrase or thought. But that word, *koinonia,* is the same word used in the Acts of the Apostles to describe the initial response to the good news, to describe the church community itself. "And the churches grew in numbers daily. And they continued in the teaching of the apostles, in the life of the *koinonia,* in the breaking of the bread, in the following of the Way."

"This bread that we break, is it not the brotherhood? Is it not the community? Is it not the church? Is it not the orporor?"

These Masai communities did, in fact, build up and make the church in each eucharist they celebrated.

Mass in the Masai communities took on an open and free form, as open and free as the life the people lived. This was to prove true also with the Sonjo people, a tribe that was evangelized after the Masai evangelization began. Mass was different in different places. The ritual surrounding it took on the characteristics of the community celebrating it. The Mass in Ab-

raham Ndangoya's community was joyous, festive, embracing all
of the neighborhood in which it was celebrated. Ole Sikii's community Mass was reverent, pious, serious, urgent. Both were
open and free.

I used to look forward to evening Mass in Ole Sikii's village. It
began when I drove my Landrover up to his village. The cows
were just returning with their tired and parched herders. Children swarmed all over me with their heads bowed low in the
typical gesture of a young Masai person greeting an adult. They
waited to be touched on the top of the head, and if you did not
do it, they kept butting you gently until you did. Elders left their
work of standing at the various gates, supervising the return of
the cows, assuring themselves that each cow, by name not by
number, had returned safely, greeted me and went back to their
work. Mothers, scattered throughout the village near all their
houses had already begun the milking of the returning cows, but
they heard you come in.

In every house in the village, the consciousness of the evening
Mass had penetrated to some extent. In varying degrees,
everyone in the village was thinking of the Mass, was turning
towards the Mass, in a sense was already participating in the
Mass, because it began when I drove in. Or long before. It was a
strange kind of Mass. No church building, not even any special,
fixed spot where it took place. As a matter of fact it moved
around all over the village. It started in the spot where several
elders had lighted a fire from two sticks of wood, even before I
arrived.

An important act, on my part, before I entered the village, was
to stoop down, scoop up a handful of grass, and present it to the
first elders who greeted me. Grass was another sacred sign
among the Masai, like spittle. Since their cattle, and they themselves, lived off grass, it was a vital and a holy sign to them, a sign
of peace and happiness and well-being.

During stormy and angry arguments that might arise in their
lives, a tuft of grass, offered by one Masai and accepted by the

second, was an assurance that no violence would erupt because of the differences and arguments. No Masai would violate that sacred sign of peace offered, because it was not only a *sign* of peace; it *was* peace. Just as spittle was forgiveness. Such was the sacramental system of the Masai.

So, as the Mass began, I picked up a tuft of grass and passed it on to the first elder who met me, and greeted him with "the peace of Christ." He accepted it and passed it on to his family, and they passed it on to neighboring elders and their families. It had to pass all through the village.

The Mass moved from the place of the fire lighting to the place of the passing of the grass to the dancing area where dancing was always done in the village. The singing began not long after I got there, and that singing was not choir practice. It was the Mass. I never told these people which songs to sing. They sang what they wanted to sing and when they wanted to. Ole Sikii's community was the first to enshrine Christian thoughts in Masai music.

The dancers of another tribe, which began to be evangelized shortly after the Masai tribe, did a very interesting thing during the Mass in their area. This was the Sonjo tribe and they were very expert dancers. They brought their music directly to the place where the bread and wine were later to be blessed, and performed it there deliberately and carefully. Some of their music was decidedly secular. The elders in that community pointed out to me that the purpose of such a procedure was to make an actual judgment on a very important area of their lives. The time of the eucharist was the time for that judgment. They were not ashamed of that particular dance in their own lives, so they wanted that part of their lives to be offered with the eucharist. There were some dances they were ashamed to bring into the eucharist. By that very fact, a judgment had been made on them. Such dances should no longer be part of their lives at all. Eucharist served as a judgment for them.

The Mass continued in different parts of the village. I could not be present for all parts of the Mass. I stopped by and chatted with a woman who was repairing the mud roof of her igloo-like house. This was part of the Mass, too, the repairing of a human family dwelling. Their purpose was not to leave their lives outside the Mass, but to bring them into the eucharist, to offer them along with the bread and wine.

I retired to Ole Sikii's hut where we talked of the people he was instructing for baptism. He took out of his precious little box the books I had given him, the bible, some typed notes on religious instruction, and we discussed them. He took me to the house of a sick woman; in bed with fever. We both talked with her, put our hands on her head and told her we would pray for her at the eucharist, and that someone would bring her eucharistic bread before she went to sleep.

We walked out past the dancing group, which had increased in numbers, and went to a spot where several leaders were gathered. This was the core of the Christian leadership in the village, and I talked to these people in a way I did not talk to the others. I lit a lantern and sat down with them. We opened and read a section of the bible and a carefully prepared lesson followed, just for them. It was difficult and tiring—much exchange of Masai thought and Christian thought. But it was necessary. Besides Ole Sikii, one of them sitting there—I didn't know which one—was a candidate for ordination someday.

By the time we were finished, many more people had gathered. The children were getting cranky and noisy. It was turning chilly and we moved over to where the fire was. The singers had come there, too.

The only thing that made these people different from others around them was the faith they professed, so it was important that they could give an account of it. A woman tried to do just that, and they agreed she did fairly well. No one could add anything to it, so that was their creed for now, their level of being different from others.

We reminded them of the sick person and asked someone to

pray for her. A woman obliged, and she went from the sick lady to the dry season to the hard work of herding and carrying water. Soon she had the whole gathering praying with her. The singers sang a song and the villagers joined in. I asked one of the leaders to explain something of what we had been discussing from the bible. Everyone was free to join in the discussion.

I never knew if the eucharist would emerge from all of this. The leaders were the ones to decide yes or no. We had tried to teach these people that it was not easy to achieve the eucharist. It was not an act of magic accomplished with the saying of a few words in the right order. One wonders how often we really do achieve the eucharist in our lives. If the eucharist was not an offering of their whole life—the family raising, the herding, the milking and working and singing—it was hardly the eucharist or the Mass.

And if the life in the village had been less than human or holy, then there was no Mass. If there had been selfishness and forgetfulness and hatefulness and lack of forgiveness in the work that had been done, in the life that had been led here, let them not make a sacrilege out of it by calling it the Body of Christ. And the leaders did decide occasionally that, despite the prayers and readings and discussions, if the grass had stopped, if someone, or some group, in the village had refused to accept the grass as the sign of the peace of Christ, there would be no eucharist at this time.

At other times the will was there to override the weaknesses in the community, the will to ask the Spirit to come on this community to change it into the Body of Christ, so that we could say together, "This—not just the bread and wine, but the whole life of the village, its work, play, joy, sorrow, the homes, the grazing fields, the flocks, the people—all this is my Body."

The leaders made the decision, and asked me to say again the words of institution. And we took and ate. And we sent some of the blessed bread to the sick in bed. The singers liked the Our Father so much they sang it twice.

Some got up to go to bed. Many stayed on still discussing several things. The singers finally began to tire and the singing dwindled. It was now after ten o'clock at night.

I stood up and said, "May God the Father, his son Jesus, and his Spirit bless you. Go and sleep in peace. In your homes tonight, in your work tomorrow, in your contact with other villages and other people, this Mass is continuing. It really does not end, does it? May your Mass never end. May your Mass be beautiful. Work well and for others. Your homes, your flocks, your children, your work with all these things—your life. *Ite, Missa Est.* Go to it. It is the Mass."

NOTES TO CHAPTER 7

1. Acts of the Apostles 13:5,14; 14:1.
2. Acts 16:13–15; 17:1,5,7,10,17,19; 18:3,4.
3. Acts 19:8,9.
4. Roland Allen, *Missionary Methods: St. Paul's or Ours?* p. 112.
5. Ibid., p. 113.
6. J. C. Hoekendijk, *The Church Inside Out* (Westminster Press, 1964), pp. 42–43.
7. There was the possibility that these people would reject the elements of bread and wine as symbols of ordinary food and drink, since these items have no place in their diet. They might well have demanded more acceptable kinds of food and drink, such as meat and honey beer. If they had, we would have had to face a very difficult decision. As it happened, they showed no reluctance to accepting wine and bread (made of simple wheat flour and water), and we were able to maintain an important contact with the Jewish covenant which produced Jesus.

8

Churches: The New, the Young, and the Particular

A Pauline and A Vatican View

It is interesting to place side by side the words of St. Paul to the elders of the church of Ephesus, as he was about to depart for good, and the words of another document dated two thousand years later, but dealing with the same subject as the first one, the building up of young churches. The first statement is found in The Acts of the Apostles, chapter twenty, verses 18–36. The second document is the treatise entitled "The Missions" of the Second Vatican Council. From St. Paul's counsels for a young church to Vatican II's directives for the same kind of churches, there is a great gulf in time and concept and ideal.

The program for the young churches, outlined by Vatican II, presents a carbon copy of the mature church in Europe and America, a church afflicted with serious, if not mortal, ills and weaknesses. It is almost as if the authors of that program were wishing on the new churches of the world all the difficulties that have rent and torn and wounded the European-American church. Of course, they are not; it is just that they can imagine no church different in form from their own. And every suggestion they give implies a continued staying on of missionaries for an indefinite time, to carry out these programs for the young churches, as though we had not been here too long already.

If the building up of the young church had been a principle from the beginning, it should not have taken one hundred years to complete the program. In truth, a church one hundred years old is not all that young. One hundred years after the church was planted in Antioch, it had spread to Europe, was being complained of by Latin writers as being ubiquitous, and was being worried about by the ruler of the Roman Empire.

Missionaries are being told, in effect, that they are not passing on the correct version of Christianity to these people if they do not build them their churches, write them a catechism, set up diocesan and chancery structures among them, establish seminaries, insure their financial future, and teach them the philosophy of the scholastics and the moderns, the morality of the Western churches, and the theology of Aquinas and Rahner.

In effect, another hundred year plan.

I would think, rather, the very first principle which must be invoked toward building up the young church is that we do not stay one day longer than is necessary. I think that ninety percent of our problems with the young churches, today, stems from a violation of this principle.

As far as finances go, it is one thing for generous American Christians to offer food, medicine, or other supplies to the poor people of the world, whether those people be Christian or not. It is quite another for the American church to take over the running expenses of the young churches of the third world. Leaving aside what this practice does to the independence and maturity of those churches, it is, in itself, a thought and an ideal which would have seemed incredible to the people of St. Paul's time.

The "fostering of vocations," as called for by Vatican II, implies a particular concept of the priesthood, which could be at odds with an idea of the priesthood arising naturally among communities which have accepted Christianity. The seminary training of priests, the division of the community into priests' groups and lay groups, conveys a definite and particular idea of the church as found in our culture, and could even lead to a rending of the Christian community—as it so often has in ours.

The building up of the young church should begin, not one hundred years later, but on the day the missionary first sets foot among a new people. It is a single, undivided work, building up the whole church together. It is not some artificial work, different and distinct from founding that church or running that church, or from the life of that church.

What is it that a Christian community needs in order to live? What are the essential things a missionary must leave with a young church so that it can become mature? What kind of Christianity should be held up as a goal for a young community?

St. Paul, as well as anyone else, would have understood the complexities and difficulties involved in these problems in modern times. That is not to say, however, that he would necessarily have agreed with the answers given to these questions by the Second Vatican Council.

A Prayer

For a missionary, dealing with newly Christianized peoples and pondering just what it is he must leave such people to insure their growth into an adult, mature, independent church, the problem of prayer presents a serious and heavy challenge. One thing he must not do is destroy their all-pervading sense and attitude of prayer. To transmit our sophisticated, opportunistic, self-conscious mentality concerning prayer would be to rob them of one of their cultural treasures.

All I could do was look at their prayer life as openly and honestly as I could, to see if there were some dimensions that could be added to it. Not to destroy their culture but to help to fulfill it. How should Christians pray? This consideration is one with which a missionary must eventually come to grips. He may never have thought of it before. But when he finally brings the Christian message to a people who never heard it, and leads these people to the acceptance of Christianity, he can no longer avoid it.

As I began to consider the problem of prayer more closely in the African context, I noticed something which had hitherto escaped my attention. In every African tribal language that I came to know of, the concept "to pray" was translated simply as "to ask for." That really doesn't cover the full dimension of prayer at all, especially not Christian prayer.

But Islam had already done something about that linguistic lapse. Kiswahili, the national language of Tanzania, is more than half Arabic in origin, and thus highly Mohammedan in concept. In Kiswahili there is a word "to pray," apart from "to ask for," which is similar in meaning to the concept in English. Africans, fluent in Kiswahili, are indebted to Islam for lifting their idea of prayer to a higher level. Not all Tanzanian tribes speak and pray in Kiswahili, however. But if there is a great gulf between paganism and Christianity in prayer, Mohammedanism has helped to close that gap, in however small a way.

Pagan prayer can be very exhausting because the people feel it is necessary to mention, in detail, every want and lack and necessity and urgency, in case God does not know their every need. Christ made reference to this peculiar quality of pagan prayer. "In your prayers do not babble as the pagans do, for they think that by using many words they will make themselves heard" (Mt 6:7).

Christ taught us only one prayer. At least that is all we are left with in the New Testament witness. It might well be enough. Inserted into the prayer life of any culture, it could add the dimension that is missing in all of them.

"Give us this day our daily bread"—bread symbolizing and standing for all our needs—is part of that prayer, a part that states in the most simple way a trust in divine providence to respond to our needs because we ask, but even to know what we need before we ask, and to have a concern for needs we did not even know we had. Like a simply shown acknowledgement of need between two lovers.

But perhaps more important for non-Christian cultures and religions is the heart of that solitary prayer of Christ, which serves to open us up to the creating power of the High God. Our idea of the God we pray to will effectively determine our attitude in prayer to him. A Hindu or a Buddhist prayer can hardly reflect an attitude of openness to a creating God—a God in whom they do not believe. And for an animist pagan all prayers would have to be directed to a remote God "out there and up there" who set the world in motion and remains at a distance from it. If he is to act on that world, his action will have to take the form of a miracle, an intervention from outside. It would have to be the highly unlikely intervention of a God who is caught in the same dilemma in which we are trapped. A miracle of a God rendered almost incapable of action, of an uninterested, uninvolved, arbitrary God.

This pagan idea of God is not far removed from the idea of God so often still clung to by members of our Christian societies who no longer teach their children to pray because they don't want their children "to believe that God could interfere with the workings of the universe" just to answer their little prayers, to suspend the unchanging laws of nature for their benefit, to work miracles. After all, they are the same laws which govern human sickness and life and death and set the stars on their course and hold the planets in their orbits.

The framework for this objection to prayer, found even in Christian lands, is strange. It is an objection based on the idea of a closed and finished creation, an idea based on the impossibility of God having any interest in or power over the creation he set in inexorable motion. Indeed, despite the fact that this idea is so often found among Christian people, it is a pagan idea. And it is a real paralyzer of prayer.

We Christians profess to believe in a continuing creation. We believe that God is continuing to create and to hold in existence the world and everything in it: the atom, and the molecule, the mountain and the chair, the rocket hurtling through space, the television set, my finger and my mind: that if God ceased to create, took away his creative presence, all these things, and we ourselves, would cease to exist on the instant. This creative power is acting now and here. The purpose of prayer is to open us up fully to that power.

The example of Christian prayer is depicted in the gospels, even before Christ is shown teaching us how to pray, in the story of the teenage girl being confronted with a highly improbable and even impossible situation, a state of affairs before which she was clearly baffled, and with which she was unable to cope. "How can this be since I know not man?" (Lk 1:34). Mary could have prayed in this instance in a pagan way, asking God for a miracle from "out there," leaving her at a secure and comfortable distance from the answer to such a prayer, almost as a spectator to the wonderful works of God. But instead of closing herself off in this way, she did the opposite. She opened herself up to the creating presence of God by a simple "*fiat*, thy will be done, let it be done to me according to your word." This is a single prayerful statement with a twofold meaning: "I will be open to your presence continuing to create in me, and I am willing to be involved in the answer to this prayer." The difficulty, approaching impossibility, which we see in prayer, does not lie in the answer to prayer here and now. It lies in creation in the first place. The very ending to that story told in the gospel speaks to that difficulty in our minds and understanding. Once you allow creation into the action, what was before impossible, now becomes eminently possible, "for nothing is impossible with God" (Lk 1:37).

When Jesus later on was asked by his disciples to teach them how to pray, it is not surprising that, at the heart of the prayer he taught them, is the prayer he quite possibly learned from his mother, "*fiat*, thy will be done." The understanding of his prayer is identical to that of his mother's, an openness to the power of creation, a willingness to be involved in the answer to that prayer. He added another dimension to the prayer, though, by inserting it into the call upon his Father. Accustomed to the greatest intimacy in prayer which united him with the one he called almost familiarly "Abba," his prayer invites us to share in that unthinkable intimacy with the Father. Unthinkable even for us. Certainly more so for the pagan who can only conceive of a terribly remote God separated from him by a vast gulf. Gulf there is, and it takes the power of the Spirit of God himself to bridge that gulf, to empower the pagan and us, as St. Paul so forcefully points out, to be able even to say, "Abba, Father." Christ, in teaching us and giving us that prayer, was giving us his Spirit to enable us to say it, to "dare to say it," as the Latin Mass used to remind us.

There is much more to that prayer of Jesus than meets the eye. He was really praying what he believed, and tried to teach us to do the same. He had already taught what he believed and it is interesting to look at his prayer, the one we call the Lord's prayer, in the light of what he taught:

"Do not worry and say, What are we to eat? What are we to drink? How are we to be clothed? It is the pagans who set their hearts on all these things. Your heavenly Father knows you need them all. Set your heart on his kingdom first, and all these other things will be given to you as well" (Mt 6:31–33).

In his prayer, daringly addressed to that Abba, Father, who knows our needs, he instructs us to ask simply for our daily bread, but to ask first for the kingdom, and to insert our petition for our needs into the context of the kingdom. That makes the prayer strikingly different from pagan prayer and pagan long-ing. All this, with that *fiat* at the heart of it, makes for a uniquely Christian prayer:

Our Father . . .

Thy Kingdom come . . .

Thy Will be done . . .

Give us this day our daily bread . . .

The part of the prayer that follows is as singular as what preceded it. A pagan finds it difficult, if not impossible, to forgive those who have offended, insulted, humiliated, or dealt unjustly with him. He would not consider himself a man, a full adult human being, if he would not get back at someone who had injured him; a tit for tat, tooth for tooth, eye for eye. To forgive him would be unthinkable and betray an unspeakable weakness and lack of humanity. It is distinctly disturbing and Christian to pray: "forgive us our sins as we forgive those who sin against us."

The prayer of Jesus is just as dangerous and risky as the prayer of Mary. Jesus not only taught us how to say that prayer. He said it himself on the darkest night of his life. At that terrible moment, when he fully realized just what it was he was being called to, he once again prayed to that "Abba" of his. He asked for his daily bread, which in this case was to have that cup, that cup of poison, taken away from him. And then instead of asking a remote God to work his miracle "over there somewhere" far away from him, he spoke that word which cost him dearly-*"fiat."* Thy will be done. And by that word he opened himself up to the creating, redeeming power of God within him, and God's powerful work would be done, not outside him but in him, and he himself would be part of and involved in that deadly answer to his prayer.

Perhaps Americans and other Christians do not pray anymore because they are afraid to pray. It is a dangerous undertaking.

I believe this is the necessary dimension Christianity adds to pagan prayer, or to Hindu and Buddhist prayer. It opens up an already beautifully prayerful people, opens them up to God, to man, and to creation. Paganism is a closed and fatalistic system. What we are asking them to believe, in their prayers, is not that the laws of the universe are being suspended, but that creation is open-ended and continuing.

It is a pagan idea to dwell on the possibility or impossibility of God's suspending the laws of the universe, and working tricks and wonders and miracles. I really would not lead anyone down that path. But it is a Christian idea to believe in God being constantly present and continually creating, if only we are open to him. Response to prayer is no more impossible than creation or incarnation or resurrection.

In prayer it is not really so much what happens to God that is important, as what happens to us. The crucial question in prayer is not whether God suspends the laws of the universe, or whether he grants what people ask for, but whether we really open ourselves to him, open ourselves to his creating, saving presence.

As a missionary, I would have to try to open the Masai people to the presence of God. Holiness for them would not be counted in great deeds done, but simply in remaining open to God and man and creation. I had to tell them, "To be holy means to be open. If God is present to you, all things are possible. There is no limit to what you can become."

There is probably only one formal prayer I would ever teach them—the Our Father. That one prayer would be taught, of course, in the context of what these newly baptized people already understood and practiced in the eucharist. Eucharist, act of thanksgiving, was part of their Christian life, and an essential step towards Christian maturity. These new Christians would first have to learn that all meaningful prayer was related to the community, and as they learned to become Christian, they would learn to be grateful. They were reminded of this in the midst of the eucharist every time: "It is right and fitting and just and proper that we always and everywhere—give thanks."

Gratitude had to be the background of the important step of bringing the message of Christianity to a people—teaching them how to pray. An attitude towards prayer was certainly one of the few things a missionary had to leave with a young Christian community if he wanted to depart from them with any hope they might one day become mature.

I would not want to teach any other prayer than the Our Father because the people were already gifted with spontaneity in praying. To add more prayers than this one learned by rote might lead them to think that Christians can pray only with memorized formulas, and they could end up spiritual cripples—like many Christians. This one prayer could be enough to start them on the way of spontaneous Christian prayer.

A single, solitary prayer. It seems a pitiful, meager heritage for a missionary to leave with a young, Christian people. But if these people come to that prayer steeped and practiced in the communal, grateful act of the eucharist, knowing that this prayer is only the beginning of their praying; if they realize that the whole purpose of prayer is to open them up, what else would a person have to say to them, to fulfill the deepest meaning of his missionary task, than this: "When you pray, pray like this . . ."?

Eucharistic Community With a Mission

As I learned more and more about the pagan religious life of the people I had been working with, I took it all in with mixed feelings. I realized that these actions of theirs and the belief of the people existed in a context of life that was filled with piety and goodness. I felt a sense of respect for the life I saw, because I could only agree with St. Paul that all nations can seek and find God, and that each nation goes its own way with the evidence of God available in the good things he gives each nation. But as I witnessed the work of the witch doctor I also felt sad and slightly sick, if not ashamed. Every single thing I saw him do, I recognized, not from my acquaintance with other pagan religions, but from my experience as a priest in our own Christian religion.

The temples or sacred places kept up at the people's expense and labor; the class apart, witch doctors or priests, the privileged ones, the ones who make themselves the most important in the religions community, the ones who alone can talk to God, whether it be through words of incantation and blessing, or words of consecration and absolution; the ordinary people, especially women, completely at the mercy and whim and arbitrariness and exclusiveness of the holy one—not reaching the throne of God, or even understanding the word of God, except through him; the discrimination against women; the offerings for the sacrifice, and the daily sacrifice itself; the manipulation of sacred signs and relics; the air of unfathomable mystery about it all. There is scarcely a pagan trick that we Christians have overlooked or missed.

But surely all this is the very reason why the Christian religion came into being. This is why the early Christians cried out in anguish that their religion was different from the pagan religions, why they felt it necessary to disassociate themselves from temples, altars, sacrifices, and priesthood.

Was it for nothing that Christ entered once and for all into the holy of holies and offered the one and only Christian sacrifice? Of course the holy of holies to which St. Paul referred was the cross and the tomb. It is ironic that Jesus was never allowed into the Jewish holy of holies in his lifetime, since he was not a member of the Jewish priesthood, which was hereditary like the Masai one. He never once is recorded as performing a sacrifice or any other 'priestly' action. The equivalent of the word *sacerdos*, on which we build so much of our image of the priest—the sacerdotal image, is found in only one letter of the New Testament. Here is one place, I believe, that the inconsistency of the Western church emerges. We claim to base our priesthood on that of Jesus Christ, and write great treatises to that effect. But when we come to the priesthood in action, from ordination onwards, we forget where we began, and we end up with a sacerdotal sacrificer which Jesus was not. We say that Jesus one time offered a sacrifice, himself, once and for all, and agree with St. Paul that no further sacrifices are necessary. Yet even as late as today, in the ritual of the daily and Sunday Mass, we still pray that "this sacrifice be acceptable to God the Father Almighty". We must be referring to ours, one we are performing every day, because the other one offered once and for all by Christ was long ago acceptable to God the almighty Father.

Was it not Christ's life-long effort, and the meaning of the incarnation, to break down the wall between the sacred and the profane, to declare, in fact, that there is nothing profane, beginning with the human body? Instead of being a temple people like the Jews, a people dependent on a temple or church building, we become ourselves the temple, the living temple, of the High God. By just saying these words, however, we realize that is not in fact what we are. Here again we are not consistent. We have become in truth a temple people once again, with our whole Christian life, such as it is, revolving around a parish church building. Much more than we care to admit, our vitality is measured and judged by just how well we keep up and maintain that temple and its surrounding grounds and institutions. Our very notion of priest or pastor is built up from his connection with that building. Many years of his life are devoted to its upkeep, and our judgement on his value is based largely on the manner in which he carries out sacred actions, sacerdotal actions, sacrificial actions in that sacred building.

In that one supreme moment in his life when Jesus did offer sacrifice once and for all, he gathered into himself the whole meaning of priesthood and sacrifice, and obliterated forever the need of a priestly caste. The result of that action, and his entirely original contribution was, for the first time in the history of religion, to enable an entire people to be priest. Is this not one of the biggest differences between Christianity and all other religions on the face of the earth?[1]

I really could not go to the Masai and tell them that this is the good news I had brought them: they would no longer have to rely on the power of the pagan witch doctor; now, they could transfer their trust to the power of the Christian witch doctor. That is no good news at all. It is not worth traveling eight thousand miles to impart that news. Does not the good news consist in the proclamation that we no longer need contemporaneous mediators or a privileged caste to lead us to God? Is it not so that we believe that the people of God, the laity, can reach even to the throne of the living God, by the power given to them as a Christian community by Christ? Is not this what the good news is all about?[2]

St. Peter described this new situation: "But you are a chosen race, a royal priesthood, a consecrated nation, a people set apart to sing the praises of God who called you out of darkness into his wonderful light. Once you were not a people at all, and now you are the people of God" (1 Pet 2:9,10).

In insuring that a young church has everything necessary to become a mature, adult, and independent entity, more important than financial subsidies for the clergy, and academic programs and seminary structures for candidates for the ministry, is the imparting of a truly basic, Christian understanding of the ministry and priesthood.

*   *   *   *

When I first went to Africa, a difficulty I had in visualizing how a priest could be essentially related to a community was that I had never really encountered or experienced a truly fully-fledged human community. I had known family and, through it, the meaning of vital relationship between human beings. But community is wider than family. I had lived in a neighborhood which widened the experience without deepening it. School life provided the opportunity for relationships based on friendship, not blood, but relationships which were necessarily restricted and not communitarian. Religious communities I had known were communities mainly in name, bound and restricted by fears and artificialities and lack of humanness and absence of common interest.

The strange, changing, mobile, temporary, disappearing communities of America can leave one without any experience of what community is. The different groupings there are in America do have one common denominator—competition within the group. An individual's worth within any group is pretty much determined by his or her achievements, talents, skill, or beauty. And even if one is talented it can sometimes be very difficult to be recognized because of the fierceness of competition present. The endowments and talents that are present are often envisaged not as contributions to a community but as additions to one's personal stature. Such are the bitter-sweet fruits of intense individualism. The concept and reality of the priesthood have to be affected by such an atmosphere. Some of the First Masses I have seen, some of the popularity and lack of it, some of the frustration and loneliness of the priesthood in America can be traced to that same individualistic ideal of the priesthood.

When I came in contact with African communities for the first time, one of the things I noticed about them was the lack of competition within a community. No one really tried to stand out in a community, perhaps did not even want to. There was no particular value attached to standing out, as an individual, that is. The most beautiful girl was simply recognized as such, and was a mark of pride for the community which produced her. Everyone would point out the greatest athlete, or the best dancer and rested hopes on such gifted people to bring honor to the village or the community. All warriors were glad they had the bravest warrior in their midst in troubled times. The very notion of being chief or legwanan of an age group was not a sought-after honor, even though it implied a nobility of character and personality. The ones on whom such an honor fell were invariably sad at the choice. Talents that people possessed and displayed were accepted and recognized by the community and put to good use by the community. People with lesser talents were accepted as such and were expected to contribute according to their ability. No one was rejected for lack of talent.

This system does not prohibit striving for excellence in the context of community. It does preclude, however, competitive striving for individual aggrandizement, at the expense of the community. It also insures communitarian well-being. Flocks are herded in common, fields are tilled in common, and a family dwelling is built by the community. It is hard to go hungry in a community when food is available in the village, and hard to go uncared for when there is medicine available there. Old people have important functions in a community which makes them very valuable and wanted. And there are no orphans in a community.

One of the reasons that the Western school system was so opposed in some of the truly tribal sections of Africa was that, in the minds of the people, it destroyed the sense of community. It often undercut the sense of respect for elders on which African community was built, when school children began to despise their naked, pagan, ignorant parents. The British pyramidal educational system lent itself to the inculcation of individualism and competition in that, at certain grades, only the top half or less were chosen to go on to the next grade, making every other child a competitor and enemy. The disruption this caused among children who were not accustomed to competition on an individual basis can be imagined. All those children who were cut off at any level had to return to their communities as failures. Many of them did not care to, of course, and fled in increasing numbers to the miserable, noncommunitarian life of the towns and cities, leaving their home communities all the poorer in the process.

When I began my work of evangelization among the Masai there was only one way they knew how to respond to me, and that was as a community. It was enlightenment for me. At the weekly meetings of instructions with any community I always followed the same procedure. In the late evening as I drove up to a village I looked for a certain man, to notify him I would be there on the morrow for instructions and dialogue. I knew he would gather the people on the next day to meet with me.

I soon learned to watch that man and others like him, his counterparts in the other villages. He was not what you would call brilliant, but he had the talent and the ability to call these people—this community—together, and to hold them together. My teaching would have been impossible without him. Whenever I thought of this community I thought of him.

During the meetings he didn't talk much, although he did
keep order. Other people often seemed to grasp the teaching
better than he did. As the months of teaching went by, different
people apart from him appeared more capable of carrying out
the different functions called for by the nature of our meetings.
We always opened our meetings and closed them with a prayer,
and I was told that a certain man or woman would do the praying. Not everyone, I was assured by the people, had the gift of
praying and was able to call down the blessings of God on the
community. Only certain ones—they were the pray-ers. If we
sang instead of praying, someone else led the singing. Some of
the best questions were asked by a handful of people, men and
women. Sometimes we came to an impasse, and I was unable to
make a point intelligible except to a few. These few took it on
themselves to explain it to the rest in their own way. They were
really always the community teachers, imparters of tribal wisdom to those less endowed with ability to understand. And there
was almost always a man in each community who was notably
eloquent. He always had been eloquent, and was frequently
called on by the community for speeches. He was their preacher.
And every community had one or two people who had the
power to take old and familiar things and make them new and
challenging, to stir the people to action, to make them move
when moving could be the difference between life and death in a
nomadic community. We would have a name for those persons.
We would call them prophets—pagan prophets.

Even before baptism I could see a pattern forming, a community of faith in the making, but not exactly the pattern of Christian community that I, from my background, had expected, or
to which I was accustomed. All that I would add to that already
formed pagan community was the dimension of faith, and on
the reception of baptism they would become, as they were and
where they were, a fully formed and functional church.

And that man who called the community together and held
it together; at the end of the instructions he would not be the

one in the community who knew the most theology, the theologian. He would not be the preacher or the evangelist of the community. He would not be the prophet. He would not be the most important member in the community, in the sense of being the one who was to make the most important contribution, of which the community might someday be capable.

But he would be the focal point of the whole community, the one who would enable the community to act, whether in worship or in service. He would be the animator of the individual members of the community, enabling them to make their various contributions, enabling the preacher to preach and the teacher to teach and the pray-er to pray and the prophet to prophesy. He would be the necessary sign of the power that is in all of them. He would be the sign of unity that exists among them. He would be their link with the outside, the sign of their union with the outside, universal church. He would be their priest.

And he would not be painted into a sacramental corner or restricted to the sacristy. Wherever and whenever the community acted as Christian community he would be carrying out his function, the focal point of the whole community, building that community, holding it together, animating it to action, signifying its unity, enabling it to function. If that community were at worship in the liturgy of the Word, he would not be the reader or the preacher or the teacher; he would be the one enabling those people, not as individuals, but as a community, to hear that Word, to understand it, to judge it and discern it, to make it live, to let it act on them. Each one could do that same thing in the privacy of his home, but doing it in community adds an entirely new dimension, the power of the Spirit given to that community to reach to the throne of God, to hear the Word of God—to carry out its mission.

It is only our experience with individuals in a group, individuals not vitally related to one another, which makes us fear and fail to trust the joint insights and conclusions and wisdom and actions of such a group. And so rightly we do not. But that is not a community. A community is a group of people who *are* vitally related to one another, persons so vitally interrelated that their very fate is in the hands of the others in the community. If you add the further note that it is a community of faith, a eucharistic community, a community under the guidance of the Holy Spirit through baptism, a community with a common mission to the world, then you have no reason to fear the proceedings and the outcome of such a gathering. The final product of such a liturgy or community celebration will exceed the input or talent or charism of any one member of that community, including that of the priest. His job in a very real way is to enable that community to function.

A parish council filled with elections and politicking and vying for position with factions and rivalries could hardly be classified as a community and should not be relied on as far as its judgments and actions are concerned. St. Paul said as much to a group among the early Corinthians with similar traits and penchants, even as far as their eucharist was concerned. "Do you really think what you are doing and eating is the Lord's Supper?" he asked them (1 Cor 11:17 ff.).

I believe we should be concerned with the same question. We concern ourselves with insuring that we have an ordained priest saying the exact words of consecration over precisely made bread and wine to guarantee a valid eucharist. The sacramentalist in action. We should take as much time and concern over the priest carrying out his function of bringing the community together into a true sign of unity and bond of love, so that indeed we are really eating the Lord's Supper. If we keep the priest trapped in the sacramental corner, he completes and fulfills his function by merely saying the words of consecration. If we free him from that corner his job becomes much more vast and important. He becomes the builder of the Body of Christ among the faithful gathered together in place, or linked with those gathered, in the reality of unity and love and faith. The bread that they break together becomes the "brotherhood of the Body of Christ, the *koinonia,* the church."

The function of the priest is to insure that the community carry out the Lord's Supper as prescribed by Christ and recalled to mind by Paul, and that the community so acting truly be the koinonia, the brotherhood of faith and love. That is the task of the presider at the eucharist. He can fulfill that task faithfully in other ways than by being the first to break the bread and to say the words of institution. There is a law and a tradition of centuries stating that only the ordained priest can validly repeat the words of institution and consecration at the eucharistic celebration. Granting the existence of the law, one can still argue that the essence of the priesthood is not necessarily determined by it. I believe there are many laws concerning the priesthood which do not arise from its essential structure and meaning, such as the laws regarding academic training, sex of the candidate for ordination and celibacy, to name a few. And there are many more laws that deal with the carrying out of the ministry of the priesthood concerning baptism, penance, and marriage.

I think it is possible that the practice of the priesthood, and the very concepts concerning that practice, might well have been determined by the structures of the societies and cultures which embraced Christianity. One culture, with its built-in authoritarian, individualistic, hierarchic structure, might well have responded to Christianity with its own valid form of the priesthood. Another culture, like an African one for instance, with its communitarian, nonhierarchic structure, should have an equal right to respond with *its* valid form of the priesthood. There is much reason for believing that the present form of the priesthood, and currently the only accepted form, is indeed a cultural interpretation of Christianity.[3] The entire body of laws surrounding the present-day priesthood have grown out of that culture, or conglomeration of cultures that make up the Western world. There is no other area of church life comparable to it in having parted from biblical norms in the establishment of present-day practice.

When you consider that the word *priest* is never used in any of the four gospels as attributed to Christ or any of his disciples you would think that we would be careful and humble in using it. When you further consider that the word *sacerdos* is used in only one epistle, Hebrews, and is applied exclusively to Christ, we would be cautious in applying it to anyone else. The word, *presbyter,* elder, is the word used to designate what we would mean by priest, and even that is not over-used. It is found in the Acts of the Apostles and the pastoral letters to Titus and Timothy, but is not found in any of the other Pauline epistles. We have built a mighty institution out of a few references.[4]

In truth, Paul seemed to be little concerned with the establishment of elders or office of priesthood, in the bulk of his writings or of his recorded activities. It was certainly not his main concern. In his several listings of the ministries of the church, it is not certain that he even mentions priesthood as we know it, or if he does, it is near the bottom of the list in importance.

Paul lists apostles, prophets, teachers, preachers, healers, speakers in tongues in his descriptions of the various ministries of the church and he adds helpers, good leaders and officials without defining precisely in what these ministries consist (1 Cor 12:4-10; 1 Cor 12:28; Rom 12:6-8).

Paul spoke about the regulation of the gifts and charisms present in different people and insisted they had no meaning outside of community. Whatever gift a person uses, he counseled, "it must always be for the common good" (1 Cor 14:26).

In the outreach of the church, whether through evangelism or social works, the latter works not being as organized and institutionalized as present-day social involvement of the church, but referred to under diaconal service, almsgiving and works of mercy in the epistles, once again it is persons specially gifted and called to that work who are expected to carry it out. We today often place that burden on the ordained priest.

The priest must be as deeply involved in social work, or the outward reach of the church, as he is in the inward action of the church, liturgy; but in neither case as the principal actor so much as the one who enables the community to carry out its functions and actions towards the outside world and within the church. If a Christian community feels it is imperative to take a social or political step in their lives, the priest can fulfill his function admirably without necessarily being the one leading the demonstration or appearing in the headlines. He does not have to be the hero of the action.

The repeated warnings of Christ, about service in the Christian community, about being the servant of the community, not one who lords it over others, throws tremendous light on the role of the one we call priest today. What else could Christ be referring to if not the inward life of the church with liturgy as its mainspring, or the outward life of the church in evangelism, social action, and ordinary living? In these areas the priest or leader of the community should not lord it over others, but be the last, the least, the servant of all in the community.

It is obvious that some change took place in the concept of ministry, perhaps even before Paul died, as witness the second letter to Timothy, written shortly before he died, almost as a last will and testament, in which he refers to a laying on of hands, a passing on of authority with which we are much more familiar. It is even more obvious that after the death of Paul the notion of the priesthood and the bishopric developed to such an extent that barely forty years later, Ignatius of Antioch writes of monarchical bishops which were completely unknown to New Testament writers.[5]

This is certainly a valid development. Many would argue that since it is valid and a development from ancient times, then the present day institution and organization of the priesthood is the only acceptable form of the priesthood. I would argue in a different direction. Granting its validity and its age, I would still see that because most of the development to the priesthood we know today did not take place in the New Testament, but rather outside of it, what we have here is a perfect example of culturization, an element of the gospel taking on the flesh and blood of the culture in which it was preached, a true cultural interpretation of the gospel.

The strictly authoritarian understanding of the priesthood (the division into the ruler and the ruled) seems to come immediately from the Jewish culture. It certainly does not come from Christ's descriptions of a Christian community. The dignity, pomp, and regal splendor of the priesthood and office of bishop (also non-New Testament in origin) seem to have come from the Graeco-Roman Western world and the Eastern Byzantine world into which the gospel spread. The monarchical bishop, prince of the church, exarch, patriarch, and the papal title of Pontifex Maximus (taken directly from the Roman emperor) are titles and concepts which hardly reflect the simplicity of the servant mentality of Jesus of Nazareth. Yet the form of the priesthood which has evolved through these obviously cultural accretions is the form that is held up as the only acceptable form of the priesthood. What of the nations that lie outside the domain of this Graeco-Roman, Byzantine cultural Christendom? Should they not have an equal right to develop their own form of priesthood? One that in its simplicity might lie closer to the New Testament ideal, at that?

Approaching an African people like the Masai with a European version of the gospel makes the acceptance of Christianity on their part a very difficult proposition. Continuing the process with a Western version of the priesthood renders the goal of an adult, indigenous, independent church virtually impossible. What should ordination mean to a man of the tribe of the Masai, for instance, a man like the one I described as the focal point of a community in life and action? We have made a lot out of ordination, but what does it really come down to? Isn't it just the outside church, in the person of the bishop, saying in a sentence or two, "Yes, you are the accepted sign of the reality of that Christian community, the sign of the power that is in them. We recognize you as such, establish you as the efficacious sign of the power that came to them in baptism. Because of you, that community is not a sect, but is a true part of the universal church of Christ, is a real eucharistic community, is a true experience of Christianity." Is there really much more to it than that?

Long ago in Africa I saw that the future of the church was in jeopardy because of the swift rate of increase of Christians and the scarcity of priests. No Christian community could long exist without a priest, at least in the sense that I have described a priest. It is only now that I am beginning to see that no priest can exist without a community—cannot exist and live and work in a meaningful, functional, realistic way—as priest, that is. A teacher in a high school or college or university who is not at the same time pastor to the students he teaches; a theologian-priest or sociologist-priest unconnected to any community; a bishop who carries that honor unrelated to any diocese; what does all this have to do with the ministerial priesthood? Christian witness in any field in which these people make contribution to the church is the proper arena of the priesthood of all believers, not of the ministerial priesthood. If the priesthood of all believers has no meaning here, it has no meaning at all.

To argue against a different kind of priesthood in the third world, and to set up theological obstacles to it, obstacles which could well prevent the spread of the church into that area, is an ignoble endeavor to say the least, especially when our own approach to the priesthood, and even our entrance into it have been mixed with so many inconsistent and untheological motives.

What is a priest? Is he a sacramentalist? Or a prophet? Or a preacher? Or a blesser? Or a specialist of the world within? Or an expert and authority in some other specialized area?

Or is he not simply a man taken from among men, to stand for them, to signify and focus for them the meaning of life of the people of God in community?

There was a time when I thought priest meant missionary or evangelist, or at least an essential component of both. For a full year I was evangelizing pagan Masai. There was no Christian community at all. At the beginning of that year I faithfully got in my Mass early every morning in the privacy and secrecy of my tent—all by myself. Then the question occurred to me: What did a Mass mean with no Christians and no Christian community in existence? So for the rest of that year I realized I was not a priest, and I yearned for the end of the year, for the baptisms that would bring a new Christian community into existence, so that I could be a priest again, so that I could be their priest. It was only when that Christian community did come into existence that I realized numbly that I would *never* be the priest to that community. They would have to have their own focal point, their own animator, their own sign of unity. They would have to have a priest of their own.

I began to see that this pattern could be repeated over and over again in a missionary's life. It was only then I knew that a missionary did not have to be a priest at all.

In the aftermath of Vatican II, we have been striving to charge the priesthood with new meaning and significance. But I sometimes feel that all we have been doing is simply changing the circumstances in which the old priesthood functions—more challenging, exciting, fulfilling circumstances—but still the same old priesthood, the same old status, the same old number one position in the new circumstances. Changing from town to ghetto to suburb to university to antiwar protestor to demonstration line to drug and youth culture does not represent much of a change at all as long as the one doing the changing maintains his position as living mediator between God and man and *sacerdos in aeternum* under all circumstances.

A bigger change than that is called for, a change in which the importance of priests would no longer be measured by their position alone, or by the fact that they occupy such a position, but rather by the way they fulfill the meaning of that position, by carrying out their function in the community—just as it is measured for every other Christian.

We have condensed all the hope and dignity and power and glory of Christianity into the narrow confines of a single individual. This is an obvious distortion. To remedy that distortion of Christianity we simply must move in a different direction, without abandoning the substance of Christianity in the process. All and everything we believed about the priest is true—as true of the Christian community as it is of him. It is not so much that priests must decrease, as that Christians must increase.

As one stands and gazes to the far horizon of the church, to that cutting edge of the church out there in the midst of the world that is not Christian, to that church that is yet new and young and particular, one wonders if that increase will ever be allowed to happen.

*   *   *   *

Sitting facing me were several people. One was an illiterate elder; another a younger elder who could read and write. There was also a woman gifted in singing and in explaining the Christian message to non-Christians. And finally there was a preacher and a pray-er. They were all members of a Christian community newly baptized. We were sitting under a huge tree, shading us from the hot African sun. We were in the midst of a program so dizzily beautiful and promising—and improbable—that the whole situation seemed unreal and dreamlike. I was preparing them to take over their Christian communities. I was training them for the priesthood.

Perhaps the unreality stemmed less from the exotic surroundings and people involved in the program than from the realization that our endeavors along this line would never reach the end of the line, would never be permitted to come to reality. Not only our methods, but our very goals and concerns and concepts seemed so very different from those of the church at large. We followed with great interest the results of the seminars, studies and surveys on the priesthood carried out in other places. But these various thoughts and conclusions were so distant from ours that we sometimes felt we were on a different planet. Was it because our respective starting points in regard to the priesthood were so different?

In Europe and America they seemed to be starting from the reality of the lack of vocations to the priesthood and the need to increase the number of candidates to the seminary—to promote vocations, as they say. Or from the point of view of individual priests already ordained, and the problems they face—the disillusionment, the frustration, the search for identity and fulfillment that is part of their lives. And so we hear of ways to help those individual priests find meaning in their lives through new and diversified ministries. We hear the question asked as to whether priests who have been laicized shouldn't be able to continue to practice their ministry even in communities other than their original ones. It would seem as if the priesthood should follow them around wherever they go, since they are the chosen ones, the anointed ones. Such a discussion, however, seems esoteric and peripheral to us. We are not really interested in finding new and interesting ministries for God's anointed ones.

We, here, because of the circumstances, had to start from an entirely different point of view. We had to begin with a pagan community, become Christian, a priestless community, and working with that community as a whole (not with individuals in it) try to discover what meaning the priesthood of Jesus Christ had for it. The priesthood of all believers was our main concern. Our training for the priesthood was aimed at the entire community. That group of people sitting facing me under the tree represented symbolically the whole Christian community, each member of which had a function to perform in the community. It was only of secondary importance to us to discover who would emerge as the ministerial priests of that community. They were emerging all right, and we were beginning to see more clearly what their function was.

But ordination for that community would be ordination of the entire community, a consecration of all the offices and gifts and functions of the Christian body—of the eucharistic community with a mission.

I think we come here to a notion and definition of the church that is of utmost importance in understanding what is involved in the carrying out and completion of missionary work—the idea of a eucharistic community with a mission. That is the goal of preaching the gospel to a nation; that is the response to the good news; that is the immediate and infallible result of baptism—a eucharistic community with a mission. A pagan community, with its built-in human functions, waits for years or centuries for the good news. The preaching of the gospel simply adds the dimension of faith to that community. Or put in a more graphic way, across the fiber of their community life is imprinted the image of the empty cross, signifying the death and resurrection of Jesus, a living Christ. Baptism brings the life of that community to sacramental fulfillment; making sacred the human symbols they find fitting to signify all the stages in that life from being born, to growing up, to coping with human relationships and living together, to working, to marrying, to growing old, to dying. Making sacred means enabling those human symbols to become effective signs of the presence and grace of that living Christ.

It is correct but oversimplified to say this means confirmation, forgiveness of sins, last anointing, and priesthood, with the eucharist at the summit of the sacramental life. It means that all right, but it can mean much more. What if their life is simply immersed in symbols, meaningful signs which are as real as the things they signify—like grass and peace, circumcision and adulthood, spittle and forgiveness, milk and blessing, the acceptance of a goat and being married, the cutting of one's hair and growing old, anointing with sheep fat and dying? Who is to tell them there are only seven sacraments? Our sevenfold division of the sacraments seems like the skeletal remnants of an attempt by a particular culture to sacralize the different stages in life. But we are haunted by the command and the urgency to preach the gospel to *every* culture, so that the eucharist can become in fact the recapitulation and divinization of all of human life, the sacrifice of the whole Mystical Body of Christ. *All this* is my body.

And that same faith and baptism bring on the mission to the world outside—spreading the good news, witnessing to Christ in the Spirit, working for the unity and peace and justice of the kingdom.

Those pagan elders were right. Baptism *is* everything. If we are going to entrust them with baptism, it means we are entrusting to them and passing on to them the whole power and responsibility of the church—the full meaning and implication of eucharistic community with a mission. It is not only what we must pass on to them at baptism. It is certainly one of the necessary things we must leave with them, besides a gospel tradition and prayer, before we can count our missionary work finished, and depart from them.

They must be able to preach in their services and liturgies. They must be able securely to deepen the understanding of the teaching of the church community—didache. They must be able to bring down blessing on their human lives, making sacred the symbols and signs by which they live. They must be able to effect conversion and partake of and dispense forgiveness of sin. They must be able to break bread together to build up the body of Christ. They must be able to reach out to the world around them to spread the kerygma of the good news. They must be able to instruct for baptism and judge others ready for baptism and baptize. They must be able to witness in word and action to the meaning of the good news and to Christ in a world without hope.

And they must be able to do this simply because they are baptized in community.

Ordination would be simply the recognition, through imposition of hands, on all of the functionaries of the community, of the reality that is acomplished in them in baptism, the authorization in unity with the church everywhere, to use the power that is in them.

And what about the priest? We always come back to the priest. As I sat with those people underneath the tree, I wondered about the priest. I wondered what they would think of the priest, how they would play back to me the gospel that I preached to them, how the priest would fit into that gospel. So I asked them, "By what name would you refer to me in the job or role that I perform in your Christian community, even in the temporary way I do it, until one of you is ready to take over that job? What do you call me? What will you call the one who will take my place, the one from your community who will do my job among you when the bishop authorizes him to do it?" I wanted to know what they would call their priest.

They discussed it at length. Two terms which they might have been expected to choose, they rejected out of hand. *Laibon*, witch doctor, and *legwanan*, chief. They wanted to be rid of the laibon, their version of the pagan priest. And chief, even though it was a beautiful concept, they felt they had no place in a Christian community. For the same reason they rejected *olkarsis*, meaning the rich one, powerful one, influential one, and *ol kitok* the head one, the main one, the first one. Their playback of the gospel and the response to the gospel saw no need of such dominant characters in the Christian community. Surprisingly to me they also did not want to designate their priest as pastor or shepherd. There were good shepherds and bad shepherds, and any shepherd was concerned with his flock alone, and there were many flocks in the community.

There was one role in the Masai community which appealed very much to them. He was a man present to every community who was interested in all the flocks of the community and essential to the life of the community and interested in all phases of that life. He was a man to whom anyone could turn for special difficulties and help. It was amazing to me that such a man, and others like him, were found in pagan communities like the

Masai. They were called *ilaretok* and represented an extraordinary aspect of pagan life. The word literally means helpers, yet it carries with it all the overtones and connotations of servants. They were helpers or servants of the community. That is the concept these people chose to represent what they understood of the function of Christian priest. I conducted this inquiry in other sections of the mission area among other Christian elders, geographically unrelated to the first elders, and in each case they made the same choice and came up with the very same word. When ordination does come among the Masai their priests will be known as *ilaretok,* helpers and servants of the Christian community. There is a clearly expressed wish to avoid the continuance of the pagan priesthood.

These new African Christians do not conceive of the priest as preacher, prophet, pray-er or sacramentalist. Such a designation would effectively kill the priesthood and at the same time deprive the community as a whole of the power of the sacraments. They rather think of the priest as the one (seemingly the *only* one) who can bring a community into existence, call it together, hold it together, enable the community to function as a community, and enable each member to carry out his or her Christian task in the community. Without this *helper* the Christian community can neither exist nor function. With him it becomes a eucharistic community with a mission. It will be noted that familiar questions, which are often asked to test the orthodoxy of theories concerning the priesthood, such as whether the community thinks it can hold the eucharist or Mass without their priest, are answered in a new and surprising way.

There has been some discussion about what is known as a hyphenated priest, such as a priest-sociologist, a priest-anthropologist or a priest-politician. This has been justified along the line of finding more meaningful ministry for priests. This is once again an example, I believe, of inconsistency in the way in which ministries of the church are conceived. Presumably the priest is thought of here as bringing necessary Christian witness and insight to the fields of sociology and anthropology and politics, but that is the proper function of an evangelist, not a priest. An evangelist is turned towards the non-Christian, pagan world. The priest functions within a Christian community.

In the African context, which I am describing, there would develop a hyphenated priest of an entirely different order. He would be a shepherd-priest or a farmer-priest, and his designation would denote the very community from which he sprung and which he serves as priest. The same would hardly be true in the case of a priest-sociologist or politician-priest.

In the case of the shepherd-priest there would be no need to search for more meaningful or diversified ministry for him. No question would arise (if he should fail to fulfill his function in that community) as to whether he deserves, because of his anointing, to be placed over some other community which does not even know him.

The "priesthood of all believers" has often been used as an empty slogan by Catholics and Protestants alike. Catholics do not want to apply the priesthood to all believers, to the *laos,* the people of God, the laity. Protestants often use the phrase in a negative way. By stressing the second part of the phrase, they in fact deny the first part, or at least put a brake on the deepest sacramental, sacrificial and incarnational meaning of the priesthood of Jesus Christ. If only the Catholic meaning of priesthood could come to live with the Protestant meaning of faithful in the church, we might yet arrive at a new understanding of the power and glory of Christianity.

The Finishable Task

It might have been the late evening hour or simple exhaustion that brought on the melancholy thoughts. I was camped under an umbrella-like acacia tree and I looked out on the nearby

Masai village and the rolling savannahs beyond. The herders were bringing the cattle back to the village enclosure for the night. You could almost set your clock by it. You didn't even need a clock or a watch. The herders didn't have any, but they were never late. All they had to do was look up at the heavens to know the time. The African equatorial sky seen from those plains below was like a perfect dome that served as a gigantic time-piece. The dome was dark for twelve hours and light for twelve, equally divided between sunlight and starlight. In the daylight, it took just twelve hours for the sun to move across that dome from the Eastern rim to the Western, and anyone could look up and know what time it was by seeing where the sun stood in the sky. When it was a quarter of the way across, it was three o'clock, African time and biblical time. It was strange how the two times seemed to merge for me when I used the sky clock. The hottest part of the day was when the sun was moving between half way across and three quarters of the way across, from the sixth hour until the ninth hour, the hours when Jesus died.

I looked out from underneath my umbrella tree with just one hour of sunlight left. It was the eleventh hour, not the most propitious hour of the day, the hour when the laborers were scolded for standing around idle, for not working in the vineyard; the hour when there was so little daylight left for work. I thought back to the first hour of the day, when the molten sun first appeared in the East African sky, when the owner of the vineyard first went out to find laborers for his vineyard. I thought back to the morning, not only of that particular day, but to the morning of my missionary life, which was filled with all the hope and energy and enthusiasm and time necessary to carry out the work in the vineyard, the missionary task. If only I had seen at that hour what I was beginning to see now, perhaps many things would be different. The hopes of the Masai people might be different. Opened up and fortified by Christianity, they might have been able to step into the twentieth century with all the real values of their way of life preserved intact. They might have been able to pass through the sixth hour of the searing, blistering sun of the high noon of African independence without being destroyed by it. With a kind of sadness and melancholy clarity, I could see what I should have been doing from the first day I ever set foot among them; every step of the process from beginning to end. But it was a bit late in the day for such clarity of vision.

For the laborer in the vineyard to come to such a realization of what should have been done, in the hour when the shimmering sun has already sunk almost to the Western rim of the dome is more than just a little bit tragic. "Why have you been standing here all the day idle?" Exhaustion has set in, and depletion of energy and disillusionment; and the hour is extremely late for all of us: for the missionary church in the non-Christian countries in the political world of today. It is missionary evening in Africa.

Sitting looking across the plains at that time, with one hour of daylight left, you see the cattle splitting off from the main herd and going into the village through their separate gates, the gates of their shepherds. You let your eyes roam further and they watch the sun reaching for the horizon, ready to reach even beyond it, across a continent that is still more than half pagan. Another thought occurs to you, a thought that, if it were carried out, would surely cause grumbling against the latecomers who had labored just one hour and were treated the same as those who had borne the burden of the day and the heat.

That very idea of one hour left, symbolizing a short period of time, for founding a church then leaving it, is a haunting notion to a missionary. It makes the dream of world evangelization seem possible somehow.

But before dreaming of world evangelization we would have to change our approach to young mission churches. Today before we count our work finished in the young churches, we feel compelled to leave with them a staggering complexity of buildings and institutions and organizations; church buildings and their accouterments, seminaries to train candidates for the priesthood, catechetical centers to train teachers, novice masters and superiors to begin religious congregations, lay organizations, diocesan and chancery structures and a promise of continued financial assistance and subsidies.

What if instead of this unending process we considered our work a truly finishable task and left these churches only what St. Paul left them. At first sight, this seems much less than we feel compelled to leave with them. In reality, it is more than we dare to give them.

As you sit watching the sinking sun you wonder if there were still time for missionaries, somewhere, somehow to be able *just once* to carry out missionary work as it should be carried out:

To approach each culture with the respect due to it as the very place wherein resides the possibility of salvation and holiness and grace.

To approach the people of any culture or nation, not as individuals, but as community.

To plan to stay not one day longer than is necessary in any one place.

To give the people nothing, literally *nothing,* but the unchanging, supracultural, uninterpreted gospel before baptism.

To help them expand that gospel into a creed and a way of life after baptism.

To enable them to pray as Christians.

To leave them the bible towards the day when they can read it and use it as a living letter in their lives.

To insist that they themselves be their own future missionaries.

To link them with the outside church in unity, and the outside world in charity and justice.

To agree with them that baptism is indeed everything; that the reception of baptism is the acceptance of the total responsibility and the full, active sacramental power of the church, the eucharistic community with a mission.

To encourage them to trust in the Spirit given at baptism, and to use the powers and gifts and charisms given to the community by the Spirit.

And then the final step.

The final missionary step as regards the people of any nation or culture, and the most important lesson we will ever teach them—is to leave them.

NOTES TO CHAPTER 8

1. Hans Kung, *The Church* (New York: Sheed and Ward, 1967), p. 366.

2. Ibid., p. 373.

3. Ibid., pp. 404,405,412.

4. Ibid., p. 402.

5. Ibid., p. 410.

9

Signs of the Times

The Gospel and Development

A missionary cannot be blind to the signs of the times, but he is often bewildered by the conflicting political and socio-economic systems confronting him, and yet he is urged on every side to take some stand as regards these systems, to get involved in some social or political program as part of his missionary vocation, as witness to the full gospel.

If there is one theme which has been repeated in this book it is that the gospel is the affair of the missionary, and the interpretation of the gospel is the affair of the people who hear that gospel. It would not be at all consistent to claim that the missionary has no right to interpret the gospel message philosophically or theologically or morally or spiritually or ascetically or liturgically for the people of any culture to whom he brings that gospel, but that he does somehow have the right to interpret it politically and preach that political interpretation as the gospel of Jesus Christ. We evangelical missionaries may be woefully mistaken in our refusal to preach a political gospel, but we are consistent.

One cannot find in the New Testament the blueprint for any socio-economic program. That is not to say that traces of the gospel cannot be found in different socio-economic, political programs. But it is to say something which is obvious: the gospel cannot be identified with any social, political, or economic system. Even though it is obvious, it is something about which we must be reminded from time to time. We must be reminded that it is dangerous to preach the gospel as part of any system. The gospel is lost through any such identification.

This identification of gospel with system has been made more than once, and in the end we are confronted with astounding conclusions: the gospel is monarchy, the divine right of kings; the gospel is democracy; the gospel is capitalism—so said the Calvinists; the gospel is apartheid—so say the South Africans; the gospel is Marxism, the gospel is African socialism.

The gospel is none of these things.

The gospel is not progress or development. It is not nation building. It is not adult education. It is not a school system. It is not a health campaign. It is not a five-year plan. It is not an economic program. It is not a ranching scheme or water development. It is not an independence movement. It is not the freedom fighters. It is not the liberation movement. It is not the black power movement. It is not the civil rights movement. It is not violent revolution.

It seems that never has the temptation been stronger than it is now to identify the gospel with these very worthwhile things. To see the gospel as adaptable and applicable to real life in all its dimensions is good. No one would deny the connection between the gospel and development. But what has to be denied is the identification of the two things. As Ivan Illich pointed out long ago, in reference to South America, we must get out of this business, this business of identifying the gospel with system, any system, or we leave to a future generation the agony of separating once again the two realities.[4]

Our business, as Christians, is the establishment of the kingdom. It is a kingdom that takes its beginnings here in this real world, and aims at the fulfilling of this world, of bringing this world to its destiny. But it is not a kingdom that can be identified with the Roman Empire any more than it can be identified with a capitalist paradise or a Marxist utopia. The dimensions of this kingdom reach to domains that politics can never reach, to the realms of the "kingdom that is not of this world." It is that extra dimension that Christians are called on to participate in making a reality. Politics, as well as everything else that is human and earthy, has its place in the establishment of the kingdom. But the political reality is not the ultimate value, nor is it the sole instrument for the bringing of the kingdom.

To accept any system as gospel is to accept the limits of that system, to refuse to see further than that system or to see more clearly or to see sooner or to render judgment on it or to prophesy against it. It is merely to ratify the limits such a system places on the kingdom. It is to turn our faith into a religion. And it makes little difference whether it is a religion of the right or of the left. Every time we have taken the gospel into the political game in this way, we have ended up betraying the gospel.

*   *   *   *

There is a strange anomaly in the mentality of Jesus towards justice, at least as that mentality can be deduced from New Testament witness. Christ is quoted and used as the justification of our keen struggle for justice, yet it is difficult to find one quote attributed to him advocating justice or the struggle for justice. The Sermon on the Mount is hardly a cry for justice. "You have heard an eye for an eye and a tooth for a tooth. . . . I say to you if anyone hits you on the right cheek, offer him the other as well. If a man takes your tunic, let him have your cloak" (Mt 5:38–40). Return love for hate, good for evil, blessing for curse.

It really would be justice to demand the removal of the tooth of one who knocked out a tooth of yours, or to strike back at someone hitting you, or to demand the death penalty for a murderer; to hate the enemy, the evil one, to retaliate against those who persecute, to curse those who curse you.

The African pagan is noted for his keen sense of justice; revenge might be a more accurate word. Masai tribesmen, as well as other Africans, feel your manhood requires you to get back at a person who has wronged you. Their whole law, like the Jewish law, abounds in this sensitive feeling for justice. If a man kills one of your cows, according to Masai law, you have a right to one of his, or five for five, as the case may be. Or an eye for an eye and a tooth for a tooth. It is a remnant of a pagan past, evident even today in tribal courts where there is a severe, disproportionate fine levied against someone who accidentally knocks out the tooth of another, the size of the fine undoubtedly the modern equivalent for the traditional law of *talio,* which would require the removal of the offender's tooth.

Christ did not advocate such justice. Nor in the stories he told can one find traces of that burning desire for justice that we modern, politicized Christians feel. There is the story of the prodigal son, which is really the story of the prodigal father, who did not use justice as his measure, and who did not render the wayward son his just desserts. One of Christ's stories is actually called the story of the unjust steward. And Christ praised him. In another famous story, the master of the vineyard went beyond all bounds of equal justice in paying the latecomers of one hour of labor on a parity with those who had worked all day.

Christ seems actually to be scorning justice. Perhaps he was, not in itself, but merely our conception of it. He knew, despite the grand illusions we have of ourselves as passionate lovers of justice, we are anything but lovers of justice. Or we are lovers of it in a distinctly one-sided and exclusive way.

To return the blow we receive, with what we consider commensurate force, inevitably leads the one we strike to feel he has been unjustly dealt with, and to retaliate with even greater force. We are not achieving justice at all but a continuation of injustice. To fight against political repression with violence leads to greater repression and more violence. To return hate for hate leads to further hate. Christ seems to be calling us to rise above the arena and atmosphere of blow and counter-blow, strike and counter-strike, to the only level where justice is even remotely possible, the level of mercy and love. Otherwise we forever cut off the possibility, for ourselves and our opponents, of reaching that plane where we both can respond to one another with mutual respect and reconciliation and forgiveness and love and justice. And that leaves the entire matter to be settled simply by the application of the greater, more brutal force.

To love one's enemy is not just a pious cliché or a meaningless inspirational dictum, but a profound and unique guide to human action and morality. In an era of the most advanced techniques of sociology and psychology and group control and political science (and of advanced military weapons), we have a tendency to have illusions about the superiority and scientific objectivity of our methods of dealing with individuals and groups and peoples and families of nations. But in reality we will have to aim much higher than we do if we can ever hope to achieve the justice at which we claim we are aiming.

Human actions or crusades whose goal is the rectifying of the injustice in the world through violence against those who have caused that injustice is certainly a justifiable human and political endeavor. It can even be called a morally justified goal.

That is not to say it is necessarily a Christian solution.

The moral person of the Old Testament, a product of the Law; the noble pagan, a product of his culture; and the political revolutionary, a product of his time—have one thing in common: a solution to specific evil in the world. By definition, in each case, it is not a Christian solution. And it does not become so merely by its concern with justice.

If we take seriously the words and life of the man from Galilee, we are driven to the conclusion that his was a unique solution to evil in the world, a different kind of solution altogether, an unacceptable solution by any political standards: "Love your enemies, do good to those who hate you, pray for those who persecute you." Jesus spoke without fear against hypocrisy and injustice and corruption into the very teeth of his enemies. His fervor led him to peaks of anger as he physically scattered the men and beasts and goods which were desecrating the temple and the very notion of religion. But this action of his neither purified the temple nor renewed the sense of religion nor did it obliterate evil or bring justice to the world. In the final analysis, the message of the New Testament, the message that passes from Jesus to us, is that the only way to overcome evil is to give into it. Overcome it he did, beginning with death which he turned into resurrection. In his case, he could not have overcome death by violently struggling against it, or by disputing with Pilate or Caiphas over the injustice of it all, and thus avoiding it altogether. It can be argued that his was a singular case, and a singular solution, and that it is not applicable to others, and to us. Singular it was, but it stands nonetheless as the only solution to evil offered in the New Testament. Even beyond his death, when we think of the other issues that were at stake at the time: the issues of justice and innocence and guilt, the question of the meaning of truth and of earthly and non-earthly kingdoms, the matter of the identity of the Messiah and of the true meaning of religion; we have to ask ourselves: who really triumphed? Jesus or Pilate? Jesus or the High Priest? Jesus or the Roman soldiers? Jesus or the Roman Empire?

There will always be a cross somewhere in the midst of the Christian solution to evil, a cross of the pain involved in not returning blow for blow; a cross of the natural, human bitterness felt in the experiencing of hatred and returning love in its place, of receiving evil and doing good; a cross reflected in the near impossibility of counting oneself blessed in the midst of persecution, or of hungering and thirsting for justice, or in being merciful and peacemakers in a world which understands neither. Between us and fulfillment, between us and everlasting justice, between us and salvation of this suffering world, there will always stand the paradox of the cross, a cross not for others, but for us. "The Jews are looking for miracles and the pagans for wisdom. And here we are preaching a crucified Christ, to the Jews an obstacle they cannot get over, to the pagans madness" (I Cor. 1: 22-23).

There is, on one hand, a moral, human, political solution to evil in the world. And there is a Christian solution. The gospel, which contains the latter, will always be compromised by identifying it with the former.

*   *   *   *

The secularization of the struggle for justice is not just a passing phenomenon. It points to a deeper reality, the unique part Christianity has to play, the unique contribution it must make to the destiny of the human race. It has to stand separate from these systems, not become entangled in them, so that it is free to prophesy and judge when necessary, and fulfill when possible. Not everything is to be fulfilled, not everything to be sacralized and eternalized, not everything to be made part of that kingdom which is not of this earth. Indeed, it matters little to that kingdom which of the present day kingdoms will stand and which will fall. It does seem to matter so much to us now because we are a broken, fractured, disunited human race. Cries against injustice and struggles for justice will be part of our continuing existence, and they will arise in one part of the human race and be directed against other parts of that same race. But our destiny is to be one, and what really matters is that we will all stand one day as a united, redeemed human race before God, in the justice of Christ.

Christ told Pilate that, if he wanted to, he could call on legions to come to his aid in bringing his kingdom, but he chose not to. And he told Peter to put away his sword. I think he would tell those of us who profess to be ambassadors of that kingdom to put away ours as well.

*   *   *   *

I believe that the gospel is the door to true, human development. The world view of ancient paganism and indeed of modern African paganism has God and man trapped in a kind of chaos. They are caught up in the powers swarming and bubbling around them. Neither God nor man is free.

The Judaic-Christian belief is refreshingly, vitally different. The whole of creation is God's work, and as such, is of immense value and interest. Reality is an unfolding drama, an immense dialogue between God and man, and will progress to its climax of fulfillment and happiness. There is meaning in the world and there is control of God the creator. Man has a distinct place and role in the world: subjugate the earth, take control of it, continue the work of creation, participate in it, bring order out of chaos, develop the world. And there is danger in this idea, a danger foreshadowed in the symbolic representation of the tree of knowledge of good and evil at the beginning, and actualized in the very real present-day exploitation of nature, in the threat of thermo-nuclear destruction and the pollution of the atmosphere and of the rivers and seas of the earth, and of the planet itself.

And there, beginning in the Old Testament, is the notion of the kingdom, a right order to be established in the world, with God as king. Historical kingdoms can give only a pale hint of the kind of kingdom envisioned here. With the coming of Christianity, the whole idea becomes stronger and plainer. Not only individuals are called to participate in this building up of the kingdom. The community is also called, and not only one community, but communities from every nation and tribe and tongue and race, to make up the one large community, redeemed mankind. All these are called to the building up of the kingdom. This is universalism in the true sense, the only thing that could make the brotherhood of man and world development possible.

There are many elements in Christianity that lead to development: God's so loving the world, the incarnation, divinity in visible things, the Good Samaritan and the Last Judgment stories as criteria for human actions, and the consummation at the end.

The two main elements involved in the biblical view of development are: 1) A love of the world, a call to participation in creation, and the building up of the kingdom, and 2) the outward thrust of Christianity from me to my neighbor to stranger to enemy to all the tribes and nations of the earth: universalism.

This outward thrust to all the nations, which is the main concern of missionary work, will lead to the end time, which is really the beginning, which is really the only revolution worth talking about. The Christian idea is an incredibly fertile idea, and has contributed to the birth and growth of many worthwhile things: independence, equality, civil rights, democracy, socialism, technology—in fact, to most of the progress and development the world has known.

Missionaries stand at the cutting edge of the church in the world, so in the church they are situated at the leading edge of development and liberation. As heralds of the gospel they remain fully aware of the liberating message contained in the gospel they bring to a people, as well as of the prophetic role the gospel has in speaking against sin in the cultures of the world, sin in the form of exploitation and injustice and oppression. They find and fulfill their role in the extra dimension they bring to the human struggle against injustice and oppression in the world. What is that extra dimension? It is the kingdom. They are fierce lovers of the kingdom and their gaze is fixed especially on the poor, the prime victims of injustice. "Blessed are you who are poor, the little ones. Blessed are you who are hungry and thirsty. Blessed are you who are crying now. The kingdom is yours." To be sensitive to injustice, to see things sooner, more deeply, at the structural level at which injustice lives, to hasten the Second Coming of the Lord—that is the vocation of a missionary.

Most often the liberating dimension of the gospel will be preached to those victims to whom the missionary is sent. But just as often the other dimension, the prophetic decrying against injustice, must be directed against the people of the land and church from which the missionary comes. The signs of the times—of these times—necessitate that.

As for the kingdom announced to the poor, the missionary does not proclaim a political or economic system of renovated laws to ensure justice. Rather he announces the arrival of love on the face of the earth, love coming from the Father. He announces a salvation and liberation coming from no law but from the love poured out by the Holy Spirit on all mankind. Laws bring no salvation or liberation. They guarantee only the minimum requirements of justice begrudgingly bestowed. Love knows no limits and is a pledge of the superabundance and overflow of the kingdom. The extra dimension the missionary leads people to aim at is not law and justice but the higher realms of love and authentic compassion.

The missionary should be an uncompromising adversary of injustice and oppression, an enemy of unjust structures of economic and social exploitation, without necessarily becoming an advocate of an opposing political and economic structure and system. He is not an advocate of any system, simply an adversary of injustice.

There will be one important characteristic of a missionary in our times. In this era of the people of God, of the laity, of the priesthood of all believers, the role of a missionary, at home or abroad, will no longer be the role of the visible hero, the one in the limelight. There are different ways to be heroic and the way of the missionary should be a hidden one. He is no longer a leading officer in the army of Christ the King, but a disciple of Christ the suffering servant. And if there must be a cross along the way, a cross in the form of violence and suffering, let it be reserved for him.

*   *   *   *

The missionary must be cautious of his own interpretation of what development means in any particular culture. Medicine, education, science, political and economic systems, as we know them, are Western. We must leave all options open for these people, choices that we know of and those of which we might be completely unaware. We must not force any particular interpretation of development on non-Western people. Otherwise, we might be aborting forms of development, still unknown to us and unseen by us, which can yet spring from that incredibly fertile gospel.

NOTES TO CHAPTER 9

1. William Redman Duggan and John R. Civille, *Tanzania and Nyerere: A Study of Ujamaa and Nationhood* (Maryknoll: Orbis Books, 1976), p. 172.

2. Julius K. Nyerere, *Freedom and Unity* (Dar es Salaam: Oxford University Press, 1966), p. 207.

3. Julius K. Nyerere, *Freedom and Unity: A Selection from Writings and Speeches, 1952–1965* (London: Oxford University Press, 1967), p. 72.

4. "CIDOC", *National Catholic Reporter,* Vol. 4, No. 31, May 29, 1968, p. 7.

10

The Winds of Change

Cry Beloved Country

I had begun the work of evangelizing the Masai with a plan in mind, a plan that took in both time and geography. Geographically it was to be an "assault" on the mission of Loliondo, a district measuring some five thousand square miles in area. The time element involved a five year target date, five years to evangelize the entire area and move on. I was alone in the work of direct evangelization when it began.

Well, five years had now passed, and the plan had not been accomplished. Fourteen of the original twenty-six sections of the district of Loliondo had been evangelized, together with several villages of a neighboring tribe, the Sonjo, whom I had not even considered in my original plan. Becoming involved with the Sonjo tribe in the midst of the work with the Masai added an entirely different dimension to the work, and necessitated a different time plan. But more ominously the *choke law* had begun to come into effect, whereby the work of further evangelization had to be curtailed to make time for the pastoral work now necessitated by the emergence of many new Christian communities. Being unable to turn over the complete responsibilities of the local churches to the people themselves through ordination, something most devoutly to be wished, the pastoral care of the people now devolved on the missionary, whose time should really have been spent on taking the gospel to people who have never heard it.

But the revision of the plan was not without its blessings. A new missionary colleague came in to help me, and, after a time, some missionary sisters. But even better, the work of direct

175

evangelization of the Masai spread through the whole diocese of Arusha. Now the missionary "assault" was being directed to thirty thousand square miles of Masailand, with more missionaries turning to the work of evangelization of the sixty thousand Masai tribesmen.[1]

The original plan, as naive and incomplete as it was, had served the purpose of moving the work of evangelization of the Masai from square one. It had changed the direction of the mission work in the area. It opened a door into an unknown space, filled with countless surprises and possibilities. In that space were many other doors, beyond each of which were undoubtedly more revelations and more shocks. The secret was to keep opening doors and to rest with no unanalyzed assumptions, not even those made just five years before. But perhaps the greatest benefit of the original plan was that it did away once and for all with the desirability of another hundred year plan of static missionary presence in the same area.

Such a hundred year plan was not only not desirable. It was no longer possible. One of the reasons it was no longer possible was the change taking place at the same time, during the very same years in the church in Tanzania in East Africa, and in all of Africa. You work on your own little corner of the world and consider your work so important, while all along someone else has been working on a much vaster scale. You find out once again, in the last analysis you are not the lion after all. The lion is God.

Today, just a few years distant from independence, almost all of the bishops of East Africa are indigenous Africans. And the African priests, once so hesitant and cautious about renewal are now becoming increasingly visible in the effort to clothe the soul of Christianity with the flesh and blood of Africa.

But success can sometimes be its own curse. Most naturally imitating the Western church in the most developed countries, the African church has not always been true to itself. Despite some impressive indigenization carried out in certain areas, the

African church, in order to be seen as respectable in the eyes of the Western church, has incorporated some of the Western church's worst habits. The need for buildings and institutions is inherited from the missionaries. The clericalization of the church, as regards bishops and priests, is intense in some cases. And the fear on the part of many educated, sophisticated African priests regarding the possibility of a different kind of priest, married and less educated, is almost paranoid. By and large, the official African church still wears a European face.

Perhaps the weakest point in the African church is its financial dependence on the Western churches of Europe and America for its day to day maintenance and upkeep. And the spiral continues to spin upwards. The idea of a world church so mobile and missionary that it is burdened only by the living and working expenses of its missionary team, with no baggage but the gospel, is a dream that is forever lost.

There is no doubt about it, however. The church is awake in Africa and ready to make its contribution to the outside church and to the world. Mission has never been a one-way street. It has always been a dialogue, and every word of importance and value in that dialogue has not always been spoken by the sending church to the mission land. Sometimes it has been quite the reverse. Modern ecumenism was born in the missions at the beginning of this century.[2] The vernacular movement in the Catholic church began in the mission fields. And the dialogue is alive and continuing.

*   *   *   *

Headlines announcing the killing of bishops, priests, sisters and Prostestant missionaries are becoming less shocking as they become more commonplace in Africa. There is a kind of blind rage sweeping Africa, blind in that it is neither planned nor organized. Sometimes it is seen as a quiet rage against the church. More than five thousand independent churches, broken off from the traditional missionary churches, have sprung up in Africa in recent years. Sometimes it is a rage against the political powers that be, whether black or white, for not producing the freedom and justice and peace and prosperity so loudly promised. There have been forty-one military coups and takeovers in independent Africa. And there has not been one instance of a peaceful succession of government in any modern African country.

More and more black churchmen are asking that white missionaries get out of Africa. They see their white colleagues as an obstacle and a burden to the African churches. None are more vocal in this demand than the politicized black Christians of South Africa. They see colonialism and missionary work as inextricably linked. They believe the latter was set in motion by the former, motivated by the former, and polluted by the former. They see no redeeming quality in missionary work in Africa. The South Africans especially are pleading with missionaries to get out of all of Africa, to leave the Africans alone to find their God.

Step by painful step we must look at what they are saying. There are a great number of white missionaries who are still involved in pastoral and social work in the already established Protestant and Catholic churches of Africa. Are they really needed there? Have they already overstayed their time? Are they burdening those churches with their control and organization? Are they keeping those churches from the freedom and justice and peace which is rightfully theirs? Are they giving those churches enough living and breathing space "to be alone to find their God"? White missionaries in social and pastoral works in the already established churches make up by far the greatest number of missionaries in Africa today. For many years they have constituted the greatest proportion of missionaries in Africa. Missionaries involved primarily in direct evangelization have never been more than a handful in Africa. In modern times, in the Catholic church, there were never more than a thousand of them in the entire world.

But what of those missionaries in Africa who are involved in the direct evangelization of pagans? Step by painful step, the questions must be asked. That the evangelization of a continent that is today more than half pagan is still a necessity stands as the basic premise of this book. Those nations and those peoples of Africa have a right to hear the gospel, have a right to know what God has done and what he plans for mankind. It is not only for the sake of those who have not yet heard the gospel that it must be preached, but also for those who are bringing it, so that the gospel, God's revelation to mankind might be fully known by reaching all the nations of the world. But who has the burden and the responsibility of taking the gospel to the nations of Africa and the world?

More and more Christians of the already established African churches are beginning to say it is their duty, and claim that they will carry out the task of evangelizing the rest of Africa, that they will become "missionaries to themselves," as Pope Paul VI admonished them to be. That is certainly their right, and they might well accomplish that task, especially when one considers the fact that evangelization is not meant to embrace the conversion of every single individual in a country or a continent, but rather the bringing of the gospel to every ethnic, social, cultural nation in a country or on a continent—a finishable task.

But there are many difficulties in the way of that possibility becoming a reality. We have taught the established churches of Africa too well. Some of them, more than a hundred years old, have taken on some of the worst qualities of the churches of the Western world, becoming static, satisfied, building-conscious, in-turned, immobile, concerned only with those "who have already come to them," not interested in, nor attracted to, the masses of ill-clothed and ill-housed pagans and Mohammedans surrounding them, who do not live in the cities nor dress in the Western way they do. The non-Westernized Masai people of East Africa have been as much harassed by their fellow countrymen for not conforming as ever they were by the British colonials or white missionaries.

But the established churches of Africa can learn, as well as their missionary predecessors have learned under pressure and in emergency, to grow and to risk. They too can learn to take the steps necessary to become a missionary people, with their own heralds of the gospel, a people overcome with the consuming conviction of Paul that it will be "woe to them if they do not preach the gospel."

Step by painful step. And the last step the most painful of all, the step leading to the conclusion that the whole process is really out of one's control after all; that there is a Spirit moving through the world and through Africa, and what control there is lies with that Spirit.

To be open to the direction of that Spirit requires the greatest openness of all: to be ready to take part, to consider yourself valuable or at least helpful to the work of evangelization yet to be done, because of the experience you have gained and the effort you have spent and the desire that will not go away; possessing the necessary conviction of the lateness of the hour and urgency of the task, and having come to the vision, at last, of how that work should be carried out—all this—and yet, having to face the numbing possibility that you are not to take part in it at all, that, in this time, it might be far more desirable for the hands of the heralds of the gospel to have a different color than yours.

The Spirit blows where it wills. Who knows which way the winds of change or the Spirit of creation and renewal will move across the face of Africa and the earth? That Spirit has been moving since the beginning of creation. The important thing is to follow its movement. Whether you or others are called to continue the work of the gospel makes little difference. It is neither your work nor theirs, but the work of the Spirit who moves beyond all of us, and leads all of us to the awareness of the One constantly pursuing the evangelist, the evangelized and the unevangelized, leads us all finally and ultimately to the awareness of the lion who is God.

Building Up a New Kind of Church

"Tedja nabo—say one," the old man intoned, in the fascinating way Masai speakers have of keeping an audience's attention, making them count along with him at unexpected intervals. There is no letting your mind go wandering off into oblivion. You have to pay attention to avoid embarrassment. You never know when he is going to pop out a number, and you don't know which number it is going to be. The trick is to answer with the same number that he mentions, in the pause that the speaker chooses.

"Nabo," the crowd responded.

The art of conversation in Africa is delicate, developed, complex, and beautiful. It is an important recreation, and is an exquisite refinement of the African culture. It would be inexcusable for a speaker to drone on and on without reference to his listeners, without being attentive to their presence, without pausing every so often to reestablish contact with them. To miss the pause would be just as inexcusable on the listener's part. The pause is an important part of the conversation.

Sometimes the speaker does not throw out a number. He just pauses. And you have to let him know you are aware of the pause, and understanding of everything he said since the last pause. Then you have to supply your own answer.

"Ee—Yes."

"Evai—uh huh."

"Sidai—beautiful."

"Esipa—certainly."

The speaker of the moment, the old man Keriko, preferred the numbers system. He was the man who, like a woman in labor, had given birth years before to his first thought in public, and had so amused my catechist, Paul, because it had been such a difficult birth. By now he had emerged as a thinker of extraordinary talent, a kind of Masai theologian. And he was a gifted and eloquent speaker.

"It has been some years now since the Ilomon Sidai (the good news, the gospel) has come among us from far away. The Purko Masai (a kind of subtribal designation of Masai, which embraced a large group of people, larger than a clan, this particular group, a notoriously fierce, warlike branch of the Masai) were the first to hear this word. It was a difficult word, difficult news. It told of the man Jesus who taught of the High God of all the tribes. He spoke of love and peace and forgiveness and of a Brotherhood among all the tribes. He angered the laibons of his tribe who did not believe in these things. He told of all men and women worshiping God everywhere, at all times, without the sacrifice of the witch doctors. He said the poor were loved by God. The leaders of his tribe were deeply upset by his teaching, and they tortured and killed him. But the man Jesus died like a warrior, bravely, without whining or asking for mercy. The hyenas did not touch his dead body, and he rose again. Tedja nabo—say one."

"Nabo," the listeners shot back.

"So," Keriko continued, "the age group Brotherhood, which the man Jesus spoke of, began, the age group Brotherhood of God, the Orporor of the end. This is the last age group Brotherhood. It has spread all over the earth. It has come to Masailand. The Purko Masai have believed in the man Jesus and accepted this Orporor. And now I see before me, not only Purko, but also Laitaiyak Masai and Loita Masai who have also accepted this, and belong to the Brotherhood. (Laitaiyak and Loita are two more subtribal groups of the Masai, traditionally blood enemies of the Purko in the crippling internecine warfare that has plagued the Masai, as much as war with other tribes has ever done.) With the Purko, Laitaiyak, and Loita joined in the

Brotherhood, the good news has spread to the whole country of Loliondo. Tedja aare—say two."

"Aare," they all answered.

"The soil of Loliondo is red, and our people say it is that color because it has been bathed in the blood of the many, many Loita and Laitaiyak and Purko warriors fighting among themselves from the time of the age groups of long, long ago. Tedja uni— say three."

"Uni," came back from the gathering.

"It was the witch doctors of each section long ago who misled our people, and sent them into battle. We have suffered from their advice these many years. But now the last age group Brotherhood has begun, the age group Brotherhood of God, and it is an Orporor of peace and love. The man Jesus tells us it is wrong to blood our spears on the flesh of other human beings. The age group Brotherhood of God, the Orporor of Christ, is an Orporor of peace, and all of us, Purko, Laitaiyak, and Loita are members of that Orporor. Tedja ungwan—say four."

"Ungwan," in unison.

"Until now," Keriko went on, "we have met and prayed in our little communities, in our kraals near our homes. Today is the first time baptized leaders of all the communities have come together to meet and pray and discuss the Brotherhood. Today, what we have called together is an *Olkiama* of the Brotherhood of God. (An Olkiama is a general council of the entire tribe, as distinct from local and sectional councils.) We are many and we must discuss our problems together. (The number of baptized Masai would soon reach three thousand.) The Brotherhood has spread far away from Loliondo. It has reached as far away in Masailand as Ngorongoro, Simanjiro, and Kijungu (five hundred miles distant). The Padris (pointing to me and my new colleague) do not stay here forever. We must direct and guide the Orporor ourselves. Tedja nabo." A switch, "Say one."

But the crowd was alert, "Nabo."

"We must instruct new people who are drawn to the man Jesus, see whether they are worthy to be joined to the Orporor, and baptize them ourselves. Like the woman Keti is doing. Like Ole Sikii is doing. And one day Ole Sikii must travel far to tell people about Jesus. On that day he must ride on the lorry and sleep overnight and buy food. We must be ready to sell goats and cows to pay for him to do this work, when the Padri and his car are no longer here. Tedja aare."

"Aare."

"We should be grateful that the Word of Jesus has come to us at a time when so many things in Masai life are going bad" Keriko pointed out. "Who ever heard of prostitutes among the Masai long ago? Long ago women were not for sale. And long ago we used to make our honey beer to be used in the villages on feast days. You could not buy it. It was for use in the family and community. Today you can buy beer of all kinds in the shops near the town. A long time ago the witch doctor would help people in their troubles, and afterwards would share a meal of a roasted goat with them, a goat offered in gratitude for his services. Today, the laibon would not think of helping you without demanding ten goats or cows beforehand. Women and beer and witch doctors have all become prostitutes. The Word of God has come to save the beautiful things we have in our customs, and to do away with the evil that has grown among us. As I see the Word of Jesus and the Brotherhood—they are come to make us better Masai."

"Esipa."

Keriko handed the baton-like stick he held in his hand to another elder and sat down. The stick was a finely carved and polished piece of wood with a heavy knob at its head. It served as a weapon when occasion arose, but mainly it was a treasured ornament. He had not brought his own with him, and had to borrow one when he began his speech. No self-respecting Masai elder would speak in public without a walking stick, or that

baton-like stick (called a rungu) in his hand, with which to ges-
ticulate. Keriko had used his very effectively.

The Olkiama, the General Council of the Masai elders of the
Brotherhood of Christ, was now in session. It was the first of its
kind ever held. It was called together to discuss the general state
of things religious, and the problems of the ever-growing Orporor. During the meeting it was decided that someone should
be selected to preside over the Olkiama and to lead and guide
the scattered Masai baptized communities. Keriko himself was
selected to fill that position.

Keriko and the other speakers encouraged the assembled
leaders of the church communities to continue with all the times
of prayer and feast days that were familiar in Masai life. All these
times were now part of the life of the Brotherhood. There were
prayers in the morning when the cattle went out to graze, with
the women blessing the cattle, and the four corners of the earth,
with milk. There were prayers said when a mother was preg-
nant; still others when she was about to give birth. There were
fertility feasts to ask God's blessing on women and children.
There were circumcision feasts with dancing and celebrating,
when education and initiation and celebration became the same
thing, and which announced and effected a young boy's passage
into manhood. There were wedding feasts and ceremonies that
took three days, and joined betrothed couples as husbands and
wives. There were different feasts and prayer times for men
advancing in age which led them into elderhood and old age—in
a real sense effecting it, bringing it about.

Keriko and the others would not know it, but the first followers of Christ did precisely the same thing. They continued in the
practice of their tribal religion even as they grew into the
Brotherhood. "The faithful went as a body to the Temple every
day but met in their houses for the breaking of bread" (Acts
2:44-46). "Once when Peter and John were going up to the
Temple for the prayers at the ninth hour..." (3:1). "They all

used to meet by common consent in the Portico of Solomon"
(5:12).

There was no area of Masai life that was not touched by their
traditional religion, and now they saw Christianity continuing
and fulfilling this process. Their entire life was sacramental,
filled with effective signs as real as the things they symbolized.
There was no way I could tell them that Christianity was less
than that, that the real and the holy in Christianity were restricted to two or seven signs. I could not leave any gaps in their
lives, vacuums to be filled by the reservoir of paganism surrounding them. Christianity had to be as all embracing and per-
vasive as the paganism it was replacing and fulfilling. In seeing
this for them, I began to see it for myself as well.

In looking around at the assembled men and women, I saw
several who, in my judgment, should have been ordained
priests. How I would have loved to see them ordained before I
left. But the church that sent me to these people did not agree
with the judgment as to the feasibility of married men, and
illiterate ones at that, being part of the priesthood and ministry
of the church at that time. So, ironically, the first Masai priest
was not to come from among these Masai elders, nor even from
the area where these men lived. He was to come, instead from an
entirely different section of Masailand, from an area that was not
evangelized, from a family and a community that was not Christian. He was a schoolboy from a different section of Masailand,
who continued through the mission schools into a seminary, and
finished up as an academically trained, church-approved priest.
It is good to have a Masai priest, coming from whatever source.
It is not proper to look at him and ask, "Why?" But neither is it
improper to look at these others and ask, "Why not?"

Unexpected things continually happen. Some things disap-
point you. Some buoy you up. One of the elders attending that
Olkiama, who happened to be one of the original elders baptized
at the time of the old man Ndangoya, was destined to die not
long after the Olkiama, to be the first Masai Christian to die.

Instead of being taken out while still alive, away from the village, to be anointed with oil and left for the hyenas, this particular elder was to ask to be allowed to die in his home, in his village, and the request was to be granted him. And he was to be buried—the first Christian Masai burial—a privilege granted normally only to very great chiefs; and his home village was not burned down at his death, as was the custom there. Christianity was destined to take the sting, the curse, out of Masai death, so they would no longer have to weep like those who have no hopes.

As I looked at the assembled elders of the Olkiama, I realized that there were some men there whom I had baptized, and yet whose names I did not know. And they did not know mine. When I first went among the Masai I quite naturally acted out of my American background, and saw nothing wrong in telling them my name and asking theirs. I was advised one day that this was very rude; that if I observed the Masai very closely I would notice that they did not use each others names in public and with strangers. They managed with titles and designations. I could get by on mine, such as "elder" "sir" or "Padri," and could do the same with their titles and designations—chief, old man, elder, mother, daughter, warrior, young girl, child.

One day, in a new section, a man said to me, "Do not throw my name about. My name is important. My name is me. My name is for my friends."

So I learned. And once again the learning process, as painful as it was, was beneficial. It had always been a concern of mine to try to keep myself out of the gospel that I preached. It was not possible, of course, to do this perfectly. Something of oneself always creeps into the presentation. In pastoral work, such a personal intrusion into your work and preaching might even be desirable. But in missionary work, in preaching the gospel to pagans, when you are the solitary vehicle through which the gospel reaches a people, and you are white at that, with all the powerful overtones that your whiteness can carry in the third world, cultural and personal intrusions can distort the gospel and even pollute it.

So for the last several years that I worked among new Masai people in areas distant from the town center of Loliondo, the people did not know my name. I never told them, and they never asked me. And I did not know their names. After working among them for a long period of time, and, perhaps, as a parting gift to me, one of the elders told me his name, and I told him mine. I was flattered at the exchange. "My name is for my friends."

For many of the assembled elders of the church I represented the only channel through which they had come to know of Jesus and Christianity. I looked at them and realized that they had had no other vehicle for the transmission of the gospel but me, and only that which I had taught them. I thought of their lives and the lives of their children which would be affected by the knowledge they now had. To have been the sole avenue of communication of Christianity to thousands of people was by no means a consolation for me, or a source of pride, in my last hours in Africa. It was, instead, a terrible and frightening burden and responsibility. I wished at that moment that I could have had the opportunity to do it all over again.

An old man, in saying goodbye to me, did not lighten that responsibility. He said to me, "When you first came among us to tell us about Jesus, we used to feel sorry for our ancestors who never heard about him, and for those people you would never reach with this Word across these far-flung plains of ours. But now that we have accepted Jesus and understood what Christianity and the Brotherhood are about, we feel sorry for ourselves. It would have been easier for us, and better for us, if you had never come among us."

What I trust and hope he meant was that the responsibility of Christianity, the bitter-sweet burden of Christianity, was now on them.

At least it will be a communal burden. A philosopher of our

culture, reflecting the stark individualism by which we live, stated, "I think, therefore I am." And if faith should ever arise in such an individualistic situation, we could only describe that faith by saying, *"I believe."* One of these African Christians, however, if he could articulate and philosophize about the vision by which he lives would say rather, "I am *known*, therefore I am. I am known by others around me who share my life with me. And if, at some time, faith in the gospel should be demanded, I could only describe that faith by saying, *'We believe.'* "

I looked at these Masai sons and daughters of the plains and wondered what possible image they would have of the church that had come among them. These nomads had no church buildings, no shrines, no tabernacles. Even their eucharist had always been a nomadic eucharist, always on the move, never stationary, never static. And the church had been the same for them. The only church they had ever seen, the only church they knew, was a church perpetually on the move, a mobile church, a nomadic church, a church never perfect, never reaching the end, never having all the answers, never coming to rest—a church on safari. For them it would always have to be a pilgrim church.

Evangelization: Counterfeit and Authentic

Some years ago in America, an atheist friend of mine asked me, "But what are you *doing* out there?" In Africa presumably. I take the remarks and questions of atheists very seriously. I think I have been trying to answer that particular question ever since. No answer to the question of what missionaries are doing *out there,* or should be doing, that will satisfy everyone, or even reach everyone, like my atheist friend, for instance, is easily forthcoming. But a missionary, afraid of spending his life in a work based on unanalyzed assumptions, constantly asks himself that question. The truest answer to the question is: evangelization. But neither is it easy to come to a clear idea of evangelization. The word has been used so widely, so freely, so loosely that it has almost ceased to have any meaning, like the word mission itself. The notion of evangelization is, of course, a beautiful biblical idea. It is necessary first to point out what it is not. I think no one does this more incisively than the Dutch theologian J. C. Hoekendijk.

To summarize a few of his thoughts on the point: Evangelization is not a call to restore Christendom, a kind of solid, well-integrated, cultural complex, directed and dominated by the church. It is not an activity set in motion because the church is endangered, a nervous activity to save the remnants of a time now irrevocably past. It is not a winning back of those people who have become a prey to sin in such a way that the organized church no longer reaches them.[3]

Evangelization is not propaganda. Propaganda leaves nothing to the Spirit, but predetermines the outcome down to the last detail. Its essential character is a lack of expectant hope and an absence of due humility. Propaganda seeks to make exact copies. It attempts to make man in the image and likeness of the propagandist. Quite the opposite of propaganda is evangelization, filled with hope, which means moving forward in a world with unlimited possibilities, in which we won't be surprised if something unforeseen happens.[4]

Evangelization is not proselytism. Proselytism is centripetal. It is a movement inward. People are invited to come to the center where salvation is localized. In order to become a participant of salvation, they will have to join the group that mediates redemption, i.e., emigrate completely from all other life relationships. Evangelization is centrifugal. It leaves Jerusalem and is on its way to the ends of the earth and the end of time. To join means here: to join the journey away from the center—a light for the Gentiles, which goes forth toward the people, seeking them out and taking them by surprise in their darkness.[5]

The source of evangelization and its necessity and urgency come directly from the gospel. "All authority in heaven and earth has been given to me. Go, therefore, and make disciples of all nations" (Mt 28:19). "Preach the gospel to all creation" (Mk 16:15). "Woe to me if I do not preach the gospel" (1 Cor 9:16). Today many people do not agree with this necessity or urgency. But more seriously, even for those of us who do, our reasons for so believing are often shaky, uncertain, and even contradictory. Is the urgency a question of mere obedience to the command of Christ? Is it an arbitrary command? Is there no inner necessity to the command to evangelize? Could Christ have commanded his church to do something else instead? Is it that the salvation of the whole world depends on missionaries reaching all people, evangelizing everyone? Do we really believe that? Will people be lost if they are not reached? Do we believe in a God who loves Christians more than pagans, or who plans to save only those who know of, and believe in, his Christ? If we do believe in such a God and such a salvation, it is to be hoped that the thoughts emanating from the Second Vatican Council and from theologians in many other parts of the world might prompt us to change our mind. They tell us that salvation is possible in Hinduism, Buddhism, animist paganism, Judaism.[6]

If salvation is possible in these other religions, is the purpose of evanglization to make salvation easier for these people? There are a great many theologians and missiologists who talk and write this way, but this is an incredible admission, that the whole urgency and necessity of evangelization could rest on such a secondary consideration: to make salvation easier for people. And does evangelization really make salvation easier?

Is the reason for evangelization to make pagans and nonbelievers holy? Or to bring God and grace among them? I have seen too many good and holy pagans to believe that. And I think we should have outgrown the arrogance of believing that all truth and all holiness, and God and grace, are to be found exclusively in the church.

There are some today who, seeing the validity of these thoughts so far, come to the conclusion that Christ therefore has nothing to do with it all; that evangelization is necessary because humanization is necessary; that Christ can be so anonymous in the process as to be invisible.

There is something so objectionable and unbiblical in these answers that we must reject them all. Where are we then? Back where we started, at mere obedience to a mysterious command of Christ? What if, being as faithful as we can to the biblical notion of evangelization, we had to come to the conclusion that it was indeed the other way around? What if Christ's power over creation were not the authorization for mission, but its reason and goal?

In the New Testament, Jesus dies without having given the explicit order to carry the promises of the gospel beyond the limits of Israel. Only after the resurrection, after the messiah has revealed himself in his power, victorious even over death, the inaugurator of the new creation which has dawned on the world, is the way open to the rest of the world. *Now,* after the resurrection, now only, Jesus says, "All power in heaven and earth is given to me. Go therefore. . . ."

Christ cannot be left out of evangelization. He is the heart of it, the subject of it, its very goal. What is at stake is the recapitulation of all things in Jesus Christ—all things, all creation, all nations with all their riches. Evangelization is a possibility only in messianic days. The aim of evangelization can be nothing less than what Israel expected the messiah to do, i.e., to establish the *shalom.* Shalom is much more than personal salvation. It is at once peace, integrity, community, harmony, and justice.[7]

The goal of evangelization, and the basis for its urgency, is to put all things under the dominion of Christ. The fulfillment of the human race, the destiny of the human race, of all creation, is what is at stake. Personal salvation is a secondary question. The recapitulation of all things in Christ is what is in store for the human race. God intends to bring the earth and the human race to the fulfillment of the kingdom, planned from the beginning of creation, with the Word there at the beginning—"In the beginning was the Word"—and the recapitulation of all things, all men, all nations, all the earth, in the man Jesus, in the Word made flesh, at the end. The nations and cultures of the world, with all the riches they imply and possess, are not destined merely for salvation—to be saved and conserved. They are called to be lifted up and fulfilled and transformed in Jesus Christ.

I believe this is what lies at the heart of the urgency and necessity of missionary work and evangelization. This is what I, and others like me, are trying to do *out there.* Not to bring salvation and goodness and holiness and grace and God, which were there before we got there. But to bring these people the only thing they did not have before we came—hope—a hope imbedded in the meaning of the life and death and resurrection of Christ. It is a cleansing and humbling thought to see your whole life and work reduced to being simply a channel of hope, and yourself merely a herald of hope, for those who do not have it.

The Unavoidable Question: What Is Missionary Work?

What is the essential difference between a missionary and any other worker in the vineyard? What is it that most accurately describes what a missionary is? What lies at the heart of being a missionary? Is it material poverty, the physical hardships of the life involved, the lack of accustomed comforts? Hardly. Many other workers in the vineyard suffer as many and more physical hardships and deprivations. Is it the likelihood of being called on to lay down one's life for the faith? Not really. Missionaries have no monopoly on courage.

I think rather it might be put this way: a missionary is essentially a *social martyr,* cut off from his roots, his stock, his blood, his land, his background, his culture. He is destined to walk forever a stranger in a strange land. He must be stripped as naked as a human being can be, down to the very texture of his being. St.

Paul said Christ did not think being God was something to be clung to, but emptied himself taking the form of a slave. He was stripped to the fiber of his being, to the innermost part of his spirit. That is the truest meaning of poverty of spirit. This poverty of spirit is what is called for in a missionary, demanding that he divest himself of his very culture, so that he can be a naked instrument of the gospel to the cultures of the world.

Which brings us to the original question of this book: What is missionary work? It is worth attempting an answer to that question. I believe that missionary work is that work undertaken by a *gospel oriented community, of transcultural vision, with a special mandate, charism, and responsibility of spreading and carrying that gospel to the nations of the world, with a view of establishing the church of Christ.*

Gospel oriented community—a community of public witness to evangelical values, formed by the gospel, dedicated to the gospel, understanding of the gospel, reflecting the gospel. Not included in this description are those whose values, vision, and goals are other than evangelical, or who neither know nor care whether Christ fits into their endeavors. Outside this description also are those who use the word gospel, but have so identified it with Western clothes, cleanliness, education, economics, and morality that it ceases to be gospel.

Missionary work is not the work of individuals or lone wolves or agents of sectarianism. Heralds of the gospel are essentially interrelated to one another and to those of the community of faith from which they spring, in a way that crosses congregational and sectarian lines.

Transcultural vision—implying a stance and a view that seeks to break away from any ethnocentric culture blindness. A wider vision, a freer vision, a humbler vision recognizing the richness of the human race, devoid of nationalism and racism.

Special mandate, charism, and responsibility—a unique and proper function and calling of certain members of the Christian community, discerned and authorized by that community, to a task beyond mere witness and holiness; a function to be distinguished from the general missionary obligation of the universal church, and from the apostolic responsibility of all Christians.

Spreading and carrying that gospel to the nations of the world—not a mere witness to the gospel in the place where one is, but a reaching out with the gospel to where the nations are; a centrifugal motion outwards from the center, not static, not an inward, self-centered, self-salvation oriented movement; directed outwards not towards any particular task but towards the one work which Christ gave his church. Setting no limits but straining to the ends of the earth, constantly aware of the eighty-two percent of the world that has not heard the gospel. This implies never settling down, a community in motion, an essential mobility. Missionaries can never, themselves, be the end of the line, the reason for their own existence. A missionary in any place should never plan for himself a missionary successor.

A spreading of the gospel signifies a carrying of the awareness of the presence of Christ in its deepest incarnational, hope-filled, eschatological meaning, reaching far beyond any humanistic or political, socio-economic values of progress for its own sake.

The notion of the nations of the world opens missionary work to the cultures of mankind, that is, to the proper field of the gospel, to the final meaning of the gospel. It commits missionaries to the urgency of forever reaching out with the gospel to the place where people truly exist, where they are and as they are.

Towards establishing the church of Christ, which is the sign of salvation and hope raised up for the nations, the light to the Gentiles, not the Ark of Salvation for those who dwell in it; the church for the "non-church," the community "for others". Missionary work should not envision the setting up of mission compounds or permanently dependent ecclesiastical colonies, but rather the coming into being of autonomous, adult, self-propagating, open-ended, unpredictable, Spirit-controlled, many-cultured responses to the gospel, which are the church of

Christ. Missionary work is directed *towards the establishment* of that church, not to the continuing, permanent, pastoral life and running of that church, in its many liturgical, legislative, financial, theological, monastic, religious, charitable and social dimensions.

Finally, the church described here should be seen as, itself, on the way to the kingdom, and as only part of the mission of God to the world, as only one step in the pursuit of him who is hunting down all of mankind.

*   *   *   *

I have known people who have fleshed out for me the picture of what a missionary should be: like the one who opened the educational and medical works of Masailand, and never lost his unerring instinct for what is African, and his profound theological courage; or his colleague in the early days in Masailand, a man possessing the clearest and most consistent missionary mind I have ever experienced; and the two women who added dimensions to the work that I was not capable of bringing to it, with the gift of communicating with people and identifying with them, where they are and as they are, in a way I used to dream of being able to do; or the colleague who was so successful at being 'all things to all men' that his greatest sorrow must have been that he never actually was a Masai warrior; and the one so skilled in the Masai language that he can speak clearly to the people of the hope of the gospel, instead of stammering and groping towards it, who has devised a scheme of teaching and a methodology that enable a people to grasp the message graphically so they can pass it on themselves.

I think these, and others like them, have always been led and guided by an unspoken principle, which, if formulated would sound something like this: "Never accept and be content with unanalyzed assumptions, assumptions about the work, about the people, about the church or Christianity. Never be afraid to ask questions about the work we have inherited or the work we are doing. There is no question that should not be asked or that is outlawed. The day we are completely satisfied with what we have been doing; the day we have found the perfect, unchangeable system of work, the perfect answer, never in need of being corrected again, on that day we will know that we are wrong, that we have made the greatest mistake of all."

Beautiful the Feet

The jet broke suddenly through the clouds as it continued climbing. There, on the right side of the plane, but at an angle from which I had never seen it, was the very sight which greeted me on my first day in the missions, the peak of Kilimanjaro, 20,000 feet high. Seventeen years had passed since seeing it that first time, and now I counted it a blessing to be able to see it for the last time. In all my years of wanderings and safaris on this continent, I had never really got out of range of this gigantic mountain of snow on the equator. I had seen it many times outside my tent, from more than a hundred miles out across the Masai steppes, pink and unreal in the sudden African sunsets. Hemingway made his dying hunter, in the "Snows of Kilimanjaro", see it in his last delirium and say with satisfaction, "Aha, so that's where I'm going."

It's where I was coming from. And looking down on it now made everything I had been involved in down there seem small and insignificant. Seeing the mountain for the last time reminded me of the only description of missionaries I could ever find in the bible, a description repeated three times with just slightly differing emphasis from one author to another.

"Behold upon the mountains the feet of him that brings good tidings and that preaches peace" (Nah *1:15*).

Geographically speaking, that description could not have been more apt for me at that moment. All my work in Africa had taken place on mountains or around mountains—Mt. Kilimanjaro and the Pare mountains, Mt. Meru, Ngorongoro mountain, and the Masai highlands.

Isaiah's addition to the scriptural image made it a most fitting description of the people I knew and had worked with down there: "How beautiful upon the mountains are the feet of those that bring good tidings, that preach peace" (Is 52:7). The priests and brothers and sisters and lay people and Lutheran ministers and their wives, who had been my colleagues, were, right at that moment, working on and walking around those very mountains I was flying over. I thought of other colleagues I had never seen, stationed around other mountains like Mt. Kenya and the mountains of the moon in Uganda, Table Top Mountain in South Africa, the Andes in South America, and Mt. Fujiama in Japan.

But maybe, most of all, as I looked down for the last time, I remembered people like Ole Sikii making the painful climb, foot by foot, up the volcanic side of Oldonyo L'Engai, on his lonely quest to see the face of God. And Abraham Ndangoya. And Keti, with her baby strapped to her back, walking happily over the green hills of Africa to bring the gospel to Masai kraals that had never heard it. And the old man who had taught me of the relentless, untiring, pursuing feet which seemed forever to be stalking all of us.

St. Paul confirms the description: "How beautiful are the feet of those who preach the gospel of peace, of those who bring glad tidings of good things" (Rom 10:18).

Over the years I had come to learn so many things from Paul. How urgent it was to let the good news, the secret hidden from the foundation of the world, reach all the nations and cultures of the world. How necessary to recognize that the goodness and kindness of God has appeared to all men. How liberating to know that no matter who it is that plants, or who it is that waters, it is God who makes things grow.

"Behold upon the mountains... how beautiful upon the mountains...."

How beautiful the feet of those who preach the gospel of peace—over the mountains.

NOTES TO CHAPTER 10

1. The population of the Masai tribe is variously listed as from sixty thousand to one hundred and twenty five thousand, depending on whether Masai-like tribes, such as the Arusha or the Koive, are included along with the Masai.

2. The modern Ecumenical Movement began in 1910 under Protestant auspices at the international missionary conference of Edinburgh through the leadership of such missionary figures as Charles Brent, J. H. Oldham and John Mott. Cf. Charles Boyer, S.J., *Christian Unity* (New York: Hawthorn Books, 1962), pp. 28 ff.

3. J. C. Hoekendijk, *The Church Inside Out*, ed. L. A. Hoedemaker and Peter Tijmes, trans. Isaac C. Rottenberg (Philadelphia: The Westminster Press, 1964), p. 15.

4. Ibid., pp. 22–23.

5. Ibid., pp. 45–46.

6. For instance, Eugene Hillman, *The Church as Mission* (New York: Herder and Herder, 1965), 144 pp., one of the most forceful and cogent books on this subject.

7. Hoekendijk, *The Church*, p. 20.

An African Creed

We believe in the one High God, who out of love created the beautiful world and everything good in it. He created man and wanted man to be happy in the world. God loves the world and every nation and tribe on the earth. We have known this High God in the darkness, and now we know him in the light. God promised in the book of his word, the bible, that he would save the world and all the nations and tribes.

We believe that God, made good his promise by sending his son, Jesus Christ, a man in the flesh, a Jew by tribe, born poor in a little village, who left his home and was always on safari doing good, curing people by the power of God, teaching about God and man, showing that the meaning of religion is love. He was rejected by his people, tortured and nailed hands and feet to a cross, and died. He lay buried in the grave, but the hyenas did not touch him, and on the third day, he rose from the grave. He ascended to the skies. He is the Lord.

We believe that all our sins are forgiven through him. All who have faith in him must be sorry for their sins, be baptized in the Holy Spirit of God, live the rules of love and share the bread together in love, to announce the good news to others until Jesus comes again. We are waiting for him. He is alive. He lives. This we believe. Amen.